Railway policy between the wars

Michael R. Bonavia

Railway policy between the wars

Manchester University Press

Published by
Manchester University Press
Oxford Road, Manchester M13 9PL

British Library cataloguing in publication data

Bonavia, Michael Robert
British railway policy between the wars.
1. Railroads. – Great Britain – History – 20th century
I Title
385'.0941 HE3018

ISBN 0–7190–0826–3

Photoset by
Northern Phototypesetting Co., Bolton
Printed in Great Britain by
Biddles Ltd., Martyr Road, Guildford, Surrey

Contents

Introduction

Methodology of the study

Following a conference of transport historians held at the Polytechnic of Central London in 1975, Professor T. C. Barker suggested that a further conference might throw light on a good many aspects of British railway policy between the amalgamations of 1923 and the outbreak of the Second World War in 1939. His view was that some writers in the field of transport history have quite severely criticised the railway boards and managements for actions which may, with hindsight, appear to have been mistaken or short-sighted, but which at the time appeared correct. In considering the criticisms, it is perhaps relevant to bear in mind that the railway General Managers of the 1920s and 1930s were regarded during that period as men of ability and distinction, taking a place among the nation's industrial leaders. On the face of it, therefore, it seems unlikely that the policies they shaped would have lacked careful consideration and good judgement.

Yet there have been very few biographies or autobiographies that have thrown much light on this period in railway history. Professor Barker therefore suggested to the City of London Polytechnic that there might be considerable value in a conference which would bring together on the one side the 'academics', the economic historians who have criticised railway policies during the period in question; and, on the other, survivors of the period who would explain the management views and attitudes which underlay the decision-making process. The Polytechnic, which for many years has had an active Transport Department, agreed to study this possibility; but a number of practical problems arose. There was the difficulty of finding a convenient place and time for all concerned; the probable reluctance of some retired railway officers to travel to London; the problem of structuring the discussion so as to avoid irrelevant issues; and the logistics of making a recording that would yield an intelligible and useful transcript.

An alternative proposal was therefore developed, under which my teaching engagement at the Polytechnic, which was due to expire in 1977, would be extended to cover Professor Barker's proposal by alternative means involving interviews, to be recorded on tape and subsequently transcribed, with survivors of the inter-war years who had participated in or had witnessed at first hand the processes of policy formation within the four groups of railway companies. The transcripts would, it was expected, provide material from which a summary of the comments made by 'insiders' in reply to the criticisms of railway policy by 'outsiders' could be drawn.

Decisions as to whom to approach were not easy. It was decided not to aim at any particular level of pre-war authority or status, but to approach both some of those who had themselves been decision-makers and some others, rather younger, who had not been in that position before 1939 but had been associated personally or officially with influential chiefs. In addition to 'company' men, it was thought helpful to obtain views from observers who had held positions in London Transport, in a railway trade union, in the Railway Clearing House and the Railway Research Service.

The response was gratifying. Only two (very courteous) refusals were received, and the interviews proved most rewarding. The tapes were transcribed by an agency and draft transcripts were sent to the interviewees. Naturally, in some cases fairly substantial amendments were made, and a number of useful 'appendices' in the form of notes or documentary quotations were supplied.

It was not difficult to concentrate these conversations upon certain topics, rather than allow them to range widely over a field of general reminiscence. These topics were, of course, those in which the historians have tended to criticise the railways. They included the quality of railway management and the suitability of the organisation; staff productivity and labour relations; commercial policy and charges, with particular relevance to road competition; the maintenance of the physical assets; innovation and technical change; the railway investments in road transport and air transport; and financial policy.

In some cases the discussion led into areas which had not been suggested by initial questions but appeared well worth pursuing. It had of course to be accepted that after a lapse of over forty years memories could not always be infallible; that personal likes and dislikes could not be entirely excluded, and that hindsight could affect oral evidence as well as written history.

Some duplication and repetition could not be entirely avoided; but in every case the comments fully justified the trouble taken to record and transcribe them. They demonstrate the seriousness with which the problems of the railways were viewed between 1923 and 1939. And when the later historian is engaged in the critical appraisal of the efforts of leading men in the period under review, it is not always easy to ensure that the events of former years are seen in the context of the economic, social and political factors of the time. It is important, for instance, to avoid judgements based on knowledge of later developments. To take one example, the issue of staff productivity which today figures so largely in debates on the railways was not comprehensible between the wars in present-day terms because so much of the relevant technology was not yet available.

In each chapter a summary of some published criticisms of the railways is usually given at the outset, and the comments that follow are based on points made in the interviews, with some interjections by myself. In the last chapter I have endeavoured to summarise the extent to which the opinions and recollections of the 'insiders' throw light upon or qualify the historians' criticisms of the railways under company management between the wars.

My debt to those former colleagues and friends who consented to be interviewed is very great, as it is to Professor Barker, the 'onlie begetter' of this study. Apart from launching the project, his continuing advice and commentaries on my drafts have been largely influential in creating any value this text may have. Any remaining errors, however, are my sole responsibility.

Also, the enthusiastic support of Mr W. H. Stebbings, Head of the Department of Transport and Insurance in the Polytechnic, has been an essential factor, for which I am deeply grateful, as I am to the Polytechnic for financing the study.

M.R.B.

1

The companies and their management structures

The Railways Act, 1921, was a compromise measure, falling short of the full unification and nationalisation which had been contemplated at the end of the 1914–18 war, but implementing the government's policy decision that the railways could not be returned to the pre-war pattern of private ownership. It created four 'amalgamated companies', provisionally known as the 'Southern Group', the 'Western Group', the 'North Western, Midland and West Scottish Group' and the 'North Eastern, Eastern and East Scottish Group'. Each 'amalgamated company' was to be formed of 'constituent companies' and 'subsidiary companies'. The names of the 'amalgamated companies' were not finally settled when the act received the royal assent, but by the date of 1 January 1923 upon which they were to come into existence the 'Southern Group' had become the Southern Railway Company and – after considerable debate – the 'North Western, Midland and West Scottish Group' had become the London Midland & Scottish Railway Company, and the 'North Eastern, Eastern and East Scottish Group' had become the London & North Eastern Railway Company.

But there was an important difference in the case of the 'Western Group'. The Act prescribed that 'the amalgamation scheme shall provide for constituting the Great Western Railway Company the amalgamated company'.[1] So, even though other railways in the 'Western Group' might be called 'constituent companies', in effect they were being absorbed by the GWR. This gave the Great Western a sense of continuity and security that the other railways, often distracted for a time by power struggles between major constituents, could not enjoy. The Great Western management continued after 1923 much as it had done before 1923; it would have been unthinkable for Paddington to experience the rapid succession of General Managers that took place at Euston, or the rather farcical co-existence of *three* General Managers for part of a twelvemonth, as happened on the Southern.

The other companies, if not so close-knit as the GWR, each in turn developed an individual character, but only after a balance of power between the chief constituents had been achieved. The Southern's first year as a group was affected by the Board's failure to appoint a single chief executive. For the first six months there were three joint General Managers, one from each of the major constituents; and even thereafter there were two until, at the end of the year, the youngest and the ablest of the three, Sir Herbert Walker[2] from the London & South Western, was appointed sole General Manager. Thereafter policy began to be initiated by a single mind instead of being subject to a tug-of-war between major constituents.

Walker's skill in forging a new corporate image of the Southern was remarkable in view of the considerable differences in practice – and in personalities – between, above all, the LSWR and the SECR. The former had been managed by practical railwaymen who had almost all risen from the ranks; the latter had experienced almost a complete 'renaissance' since the Managing Committee had in 1899 taken over the conduct of the former competing systems of the South Eastern Railway and the London Chatham & Dover Railway. There were very able and educated men at the head of the SECR, a fact which was fully recognised by Walker in building up his new team. He refused to allow loyalty to his own former company to affect his judgement of what would be best for the new Southern Railway.

The LNER sidestepped the problem of power struggles by adopting a strongly decentralised organisation that did the least possible damage to personal susceptibilities and interfered least – at any rate for several years – with existing practices. But it could be said, certainly, that the North Eastern Railway influence was predominant. The NER moreover became an Area of the new LNER, whereas the Great Northern, the

Great Central and the Great Eastern were merged in the new Southern Area. Management too, in the person of the Chief General Manager and his headquarters team, seemed to have a strong NER element. But the toleration of former company practices, which some critics considered excessive, softened resentment until eventually loyalty to the LNER began to replace loyalty to its predecessors.

The problems of welding former competitors into a new, unified group were most acute on the LMS. Not merely commercial competition but deep differences of outlook and of technical practice separated the London & North Western and the Midland in England, the Caledonian and the Glasgow & South Western in Scotland. The solution favoured by the LMS Board and the General Manager was far removed from that adopted by the LNER; it was to enforce standardisation and hope that this would create a new 'LMS' quickly.

Unfortunately where, as often happened, the new standards were simply those of one constituent, there was resentment among the staff whose loyalties had lain elsewhere. And the chief officers for several years seemed more concerned to perpetuate the practices with which they had grown up, and to enforce them upon the whole system, than to ease the transition. So the changes were seen in terms of Midland operating practice, for instance, being enforced upon former LNWR departments and officers; and in Scotland the Caledonian seemed to be trampling over its old rival, the GSWR.

These sterile struggles lasted some four years, until a new era for the LMS was inaugurated when Sir Guy Granet[3] brought in Sir Josiah Stamp[4] from Imperial Chemical Industries to apply to railway management one of the most formidable intellects of the period, equally distinguished in government administration, business organisation and economic theory.

After the new groups had established four distinct corporate identities, it was clear that the Railways Act had not really provided a framework for what might have seemed to be the logical next step, namely unification. There were of course instances of co-ordination of technical standards, which were nothing to do with the 1921 Act. Even here, there had been problems in through working because some companies had inherited the use of the air brake and others the vacuum; worse still, in the latter case the Great Western departed from the general practice by working to 25 in. of vacuum as against the more usual 20 in., which sometimes created difficulties in making up trains of mixed GWR and non-GWR vehicles. The Railway Clearing House had been the forum within which progress towards standard practice in technical, operating and commercial matters had been sought, sometimes with success and sometimes without.

Historians who have discussed railway policy between the wars may have assumed too easily that there was such a thing as 'railway' policy. The different views of the company representatives at inter-company meetings, and different ways in which agreed policy decisions were actually carried out, need to be studied and the matters in which full agreement was reached distinguished from those in which company practices continued to differ.

Differences in outlook must to some extent have been based on different circumstances. The LMS, for instance, had a capital expenditure at the grouping that was almost three times that of the Southern, and it had 6,911 miles of route open for traffic in 1923 against the Southern's 2,153. On the other hand, between 1923 and 1937 the Southern had increased its electrified route mileage by 460 but the LMS by only ten miles. Whereas the LMS drew much more than half its traffic receipts from freight, the Southern drew only one-quarter. The LMS in March 1924 employed a staff of 274,523; the Southern only 70,484. The Southern's stock of wagons was less than one-eighth of the huge fleet owned by the LMS.

Whilst the Great Western never paid less than 3 per cent on its ordinary stock (with the occasional assistance of a modest transfer from reserves), the LNER never paid anything at all on its deferred ordinary stock and only once or twice a minuscule payment on the preferred ordinary; its preference dividends in many years were in arrears.

Perhaps the best way to illustrate the physical – if not the historical or the economic – differences between the companies is to translate the principal statistics into index numbers, taking the LMS, the largest company, as 100, in the year 1923.

Table 1
The grouped companies, 1923 (LMS = 100)

	LNER	*GWR*	*SR*
Capital expenditure	77·4	38·3	33·9
Route-miles of line open for traffic	93·3	54·6	31·2
Steam locomotives	71·8	38·3	21·9
Passenger carriages	72·8	34·4	38·0
Wagons	93·3	28·2	11·7
Traffic receipts:			
Passengers	67·3	40·8	56·9
Freight (excluding coal, etc.)	65·9	33·3	14·4
Coal. etc.	77·3	42·4	12·1
Staff employed[a]	75·6	42·7	25·7

a March 1924 Census of Railway Staff.
Source: Ministry of Transport, *Railway Returns* statistics.

How far were these differences in scale of operations – and in character of operations – reflected in differing organisations? There was a fair degree of similarity so far as Board structure and its relations with management were concerned; but at lower levels, although the nomenclature of departments and the titles of officers might be similar, there were marked divergences in practice.

At the highest level, the traditional system of Boards composed of non-executive, part-time directors, headed by a Chairman who was also (nominally at least) part-time, and who was certainly supposed to be non-executive, held sway. The concept of a Managing Director, i.e. of a chief executive who also had a seat on the Board, was not favoured, except on the LMS after the office of Chairman and President had been combined in 1927, in the person of Sir Josiah (later Lord) Stamp.[5]

The government's 1920 proposal for representatives of both workers and managements to have seats on the Boards had met with opposition not merely (as might have been expected) from the Railway Companies'

Association, representing the pre-grouping Boards, but also, less predictably, from the railway trade unions. Involvement of union representatives in policy decisions, yet only with a minority interest, was not acceptable. The government accordingly withdrew this clause from the Bill laid before Parliament.

So the traditional pattern of a separation between direction, guided by a Board through its Chairman, and management headed by a General Manager or chief executive responsible to the Board but not a member of it, remained the standard after grouping.

This principle was not, so far as the records show, criticised to any significant extent. For instance, the Royal Commission on Transport in its Final Report[6] had no adverse comment – in fact no comment at all – on the organisation of the companies. It was, however, sometimes suggested that the Boards were too large. The maximum number of directors laid down in the Second Schedule to the Railways Act was twenty-eight for the LMS and the LNER, twenty-five for the GWR and twenty-one for the Southern. A Labour Party report of 1939 had referred to 'unwieldy and unimaginative directorates'.[7] But the actual existence of Boards was criticised by left-wing writers mainly as a symbol of the private-enterprise structure that should be replaced by nationalisation, rather than as a specifically inefficient component in the organisation.

Some play was made with the fact that the total amount of railway directors' fees in 1937 came to £88,000, and in a House of Commons debate that year a Labour Party spokesman argued that this was an excessive charge for their services. At shareholders' meetings, too, there were occasional grumbles. Sir Josiah Stamp once adroitly parried criticisms of his salary by pointing out that it represented the price of one ham sandwich a year from each shareholder.

The formal organisation was perhaps less significant than the interplay of personalities as between Boards and managements. At the outset, one must ask whether the Boards controlled policy in any meaningful sense of that word. So far as capital expenditure was concerned, an LNER view was strongly affirmative. 'The Board had to authorise almost every considerable item of expenditure, whether it was on new works, new rolling stock, the renewal of track and so on. There wasn't very much delegation of authority to spend money, and even the increases of salaries to officers, senior and junior, had to be authorised by the Board. But I would not be disposed to say that any of it was unwise or unsuitable.'[8]

Each company of course had its own style of management and its traditions defining the relationship between Board and management. The LNER started with a Chairman, William Whitelaw,[9] who came from the North British Railway, where he had been accustomed to talk to officers and interest himself in the details of railway management. 'Whitelaw . . . was a great man for riding on locomotives and that kind of thing.'[10] However, 'I doubt if he ever had the capacity to go into the really important things of railway management with railway managers.'[11]

But if the LNER Chairman did not dominate the Chief General Manager, Sir Ralph Wedgwood,[12] the individual Board members probably played a more important role than they did on some other railways. 'The LNER Board functioned . . . very strongly through the committees. There were local contacts between the Directors and the Divisional Managers, divisional officers . . . and of course some of the directors had a highly specialised interest in various aspects of the railway work . . . Some of the others were . . . only in for territorial reasons or for historical or even political reasons.'[13]

The last point is significant, because the 'railway interest' (as G. Alderman has described it[14]) survived between the wars. The Railway Clerks' Association in 1938 drew attention to the fact that no fewer than twenty-four directors of the four main-line railway companies were members of the House of Lords, and eleven were members of the House of Commons – in total constituting a strong railway 'lobby'.

Returning to the theme of personal relationships transcending formal patterns of organisation, it is clear that the decentralisation of the LNER, especially with individual directors acting as chairmen of the three Area Boards and thus having a direct relationship with the Divisional General Managers, could have created problems of overlapping and conflict had not both Whitelaw and Wedgwood apparently been imbued with mutual respect and a disinclination to trespass upon each other's field of activity. This may not have been the case at the outset. One comment was: 'I was in R.L.W.'s office from 1924 to 1926. Parkinson, a friend of mine and R.L.W.'s personal clerk at the time, told me that W.W. did try to interfere at the start but was quickly told by R.L.W. that, although he was the Chairman, R.L.W. was CGM and his preserves were not to be trespassed upon. There was no further trouble.'[15] But the Chief General Manager was in some ways more remote from the staff on the ground than any other chief executive except perhaps Stamp on the LMS. 'I very rarely was able to detect the hand of Wedgwood and very seldom met the person of Wedgwood.'[16]

Sir Ronald Matthews,[17] his successor, had a different relationship with Sir Charles Newton,[18] who succeeded Wedgwood as Chief General Manager. Matthews had a keen brain and a strong personality. He did not scruple to clash on occasion with Newton, even in public. 'I have a vivid memory of the Chief General Manager, in the presence of me and other officers of not terribly high rank at that time, being humiliated and just turning it off with a laugh.'[19]

On the Great Western, at least two major clashes between General Manager and Chairman did take place. In one case the Chairman (Viscount Churchill)[20] appears to have come out on top. 'I have been told that there were frictions and disagreements between [Sir Felix] Pole[21] [the General Manager] and the Chairman which resulted in [Pole's] departure . . . the episode underlines the extreme importance of the personal relationship between the Chairman and the General Manager. The Chairman took a very active interest and was at Paddington about three days a week.'[22]

But a later Chairman/General Manager clash at Paddington had the opposite result. 'When [Sir James] Milne[23] quarrelled with [Sir Charles] Hambro[24] at Paddington . . . Hambro went through the window, not Milne.'[25]

The GWR General Manager may have had on occasion to tread delicately on account of the direct relationship between the Board – especially the Locomotive Committee – and some chief officers – especially the Chief Mechanical Engineer. Although there was frequent contact between the General Manager and the departmental officers, the Secretary and, usually, the Chief Accountant were also Board officers in their own right. The other chief departmental officers attended the meetings of the various Board committees and 'both the Civil Engineer and the CME had by tradition a strong degree of independence, but I do not recollect any clashes on this account ... one should not underestimate the contribution made by the Chief Legal Adviser, both in his parliamentary and other capacities.'[26]

The independence of chief departmental officers was apparently a problem, speedily settled, on the LNER. 'R.L.W. had a few brushes in the early days with C. L. Edwards, the first Chief Accountant of the LNER, and also with Nigel Gresley, both of whom had had access to the Great Northern Railway Board, but R.L.W. soon put them in their place. That may be why Edwards soon left.'[27]

Felix Pole's autobiography refers to over-centralisation on the GWR. 'For example, the distribution of rolling stock was arranged at headquarters by the Superintendent of the Line. Theoretically, if not actually, no station master or local officer could make use of a wagon or coach without authority from headquarters.'[28] In the 1920s, however, Rolling Stock Inspectors came under the Divisional Superintendents, so that this degree of over-centralisation had been recognised and corrected.

The relationship between the General Manager and the Board seems to have been most clearly defined on the Southern. Sir Herbert Walker is quoted as saying that 'a railway needed a Chairman who was totally divorced from the management, a banker perhaps; and had the professional railwaymen to run the railway'.[29] Walker was also reported as saying, 'It was always helpful to me to know that I had got strong and intelligent men as Chairmen of the Board, because from time to time I would need to go to them and say, "I have a feeling that we should do so-and-so, what do you think about that?" I did not ask them about the technical side. They would not have expected me to.'[30]

Walker was apparently happy to know that 'there were other powerful men on the Board'[31] because 'It was a very tight concept; no member of the Board was allowed to go off on his own and speak to an officer without Walker knowing. If he did, he was quickly brought to book . . . through the Chairman.'[32]

The problem of potential conflict between a Chairman and his General Manager could of course not arise on the LMS after Sir Josiah Stamp was appointed President of the Executive in January 1926, and soon afterwards also Chairman of the company. This arrangement did not commend itself to Sir Herbert Walker. He disagreed with the principle involved. 'Walker said to me, "Stamp had a fine brain and he brought discipline to the LMS but he didn't know how to use it and he chose an American system which didn't work." '[33] An inside view within the LMS also revealed reservations about the Stamp style of management. 'He went to America when he came and found the American system of producing Vice-Presidents and he introduced it . . . It turned out to be a fundamental weakness and when the war came, of course, it was not any good. It was not any good for conducting the show.'[34]

In other words, Stamp did not personally manage the LMS in the way that Walker managed the Southern. 'Stamp worked in the existing machine when he came in. He improved it . . . The LMS was run by an executive committee and still was run by it when he sat in the chair . . . Stamp was a great believer in the ability to steer the show and also in the ability of the people on the show to work in a team . . . This was Stamp's mistake. He thought that to be able to work in a team was the best thing, the acme, the test of everything . . . If you got one that did not, that was a misfit, he avoided him . . .'[35]

Even so, many people considered the LMS over-centralised. 'The LMS was undoubtedly the over-centralised organisation of a bureaucratic kind, unrelieved by the pressures of Parliament and public opinion which can check the worst faults of similar manifestations in government departments.'[36]

Within this huge bureaucracy it would seem that Stamp 'tended to be rather a remote figure. On the other hand the Vice-Presidents were very much in evidence'.[37] This was probably inevitable in view of Stamp's role as Chairman and also his widespread interests outside the railway. It was a great contrast to Walker, whose personality seems to have been felt everywhere on the Southern. 'Walker was something by himself, as a man of stature and yet as a practical manager.'[38]

To sum up, it appears that throughout the period the influence of Chairmen and Boards upon management varied considerably, partly through the formal organisation adopted, partly through custom and tradition, partly through the interaction of personalities. By and large, however, those interviewed were not inclined to think that any different system, such as a Board including full-time executive directors, would have had significant advantages.

Where railway organisation was the subject of written studies, these were usually factual and descriptive, rather than critical.[39] It is thus interesting that in his textbook C. E. R. Sherrington[40] devoted a chapter to 'Internal Organisation' in which he discussed some basic principles from a practical rather than a theoretical standpoint. He was himself a railway employee, as Secretary of the Railway Research Service; but he was able to comment with some freedom, since he did not owe allegiance to any single company. His study opened by contrasting the view that 'the function of any organisation scheme is to find the most suitable pigeon-holes for the personnel available' with the opposite attitude 'which looks upon the scheme of organisation as all-important'. He concluded that 'the true position probably lies about midway between these two extremes'.

Sherrington then discussed the devolution of authority under a departmental (i.e. a functional) system and contrasted it with a divisional (i.e. a federal or geographical) system. 'The theory lying behind the principle of the Departmental organization is that the technical railway officer should report to a chief who is also technically skilled, thus a local District Operating Superintendent should report to a Divisional Operating Superintendent, and a local District Goods Manager should report to the Divisional Goods Manager. The principle is good, but it leads to great difficulties as the railway systems become larger.

'If friction between two departments exists, and in case the superior officers back up their local representatives, no decision can be given until the problem for solution reaches the General Manager.

'The Divisional system was designed to obviate these difficulties . . .

the basis is to subdivide responsibility not upon the principle of departmental authority but to rely so far as possible on territorial subdivision. Amongst the advantages of such a system are the prevention of a local interdepartmental dispute reaching very far up the organization. The Divisional system tends also to give officers a better all-round training, although it often necessitates a technical assistant reporting to a non-technical chief. One of its greatest advantages is the greater choice it gives of officers skilled to undertake the position of General Manager.'[41]

Sherrington thus implied some criticism of the railways which relied most heavily upon the traditional system, above all the Great Western, whose organisation, he observed, was the nearest to the typical 'departmental' one. But those with experience of it would not agree that it was inappropriate. 'It was an efficient system of management with a simple structure compared with organisations we have had since. You had your General Manager and his chief officers. They conferred and decisions on day-to-day matters were arrived at straight away without a lot of paperwork. Decisions on major policy were kept for the Board. The recorded minutes of the Board and of the Committees were a model of brevity.'[42]

Sherrington made one general criticism, that 'the revenue-producing departments have always possessed greater power on British railways than on those abroad, where the general tendency has been to concentrate attention on the reduction of costs, allowing the automatic development of the country to supply the additional traffic . . . no British railway possesses an appointment equivalent to that of Vice-President of Transportation, who is responsible for co-ordinating the revenue-producing and operating expenditure sides of railway work, and balancing the advantages of the costs of obtaining new traffic against the additional revenue to be derived thereby'.[43]

Guarded agreement to this came in one 'inside' comment. 'This business of delegation of responsibility or organisation of function below headquarters is probably the greatest problem that the railways have considered for a century and a half and never really solved.'[44]

Sherrington by implication favoured the LNER organisation, with its extensive devolution of day-to-day management functions to geographical Areas, each co-ordinated and guided by a Divisional General Manager. It came in fact very close to his theoretical outline of a 'divisional' structure. But not everyone with experience of the LNER organisation in practice supported this view. 'I thought the LNER organisation for speed of decision was abominably slow; but on the other hand, because of the Divisions we had – four to begin with, and later three – it became a matter of some chance which of the differing policies that were being pursued by these four emperors would become the predominant ones, so I was a bit hesitant in going out for central authority when I didn't know who the authority would be. This is always the problem when you look at this kind of thing. But I feel sure myself that there should, in the interests of straight thinking and an unemotive approach to things, have been more central authority exercised on the LNER. That is not to say that they failed in many things that they ought to have done, but they were slower in carrying them out – in some cases, anyway.'[45]

On the other hand the LNER's looser structure produced some of the virtues of variety, and – very important – encouragement for people to put forward unorthodox views. 'Behind it all there was a faith – perhaps a blind faith – right at the top of the LNER structure in the value of having more than one opinion and for people to rub against each other and to be inspired to put forward their full argument in support of the case. I believe there was a certain amount of wisdom in this, indeed a deal of wisdom, and I think it stems from the attitude of R. L. Wedgwood and R. Bell, who were great believers in the virtues of competition, and they liked their own authorities to be in competition with each other, so that they were putting forward points of view and trying to reconcile them before they went to meet other companies.'[46]

This atmosphere of debate and discussion was very different from that which prevailed on the LMS. 'With the departmental organisation, where you had the chap immediately ahead of you and then first remove, second remove, third remove – departmental experts right the way to the top – centralisation is bound to be more severe, discipline is bound to be more severe, junior officers more frightened of making mistakes, and you only learn from your mistakes.'[47]

Another former LNER officer argued that 'the differences often enabled the best to come to the top'.[48] Yet Area management could have practical disadvantages. 'I had the experience of being a District Passenger Manager at Leeds, responsible for half my stations to the North Eastern Area and the other half to the Southern Area, and my two Passenger Managers did not always see eye to eye by any manner of means. Of course you can say that you are in a position to play them off against each other, which in a sense I was, but I would have liked to have seen more of an all-line organisation.'[49]

This was not a universal view. 'I was an Assistant in Leeds, 1926–33, and for six of these years we were in both the North Eastern and Southern Areas. It worked like a charm. No difficulties whatsoever and much advantage.'[50]

Certain LNER departments – notably those of the Chief Mechanical Engineer and the Chief Accountant – had always been outside the area organisation, reporting direct to the Chief General Manager and not through the Divisional General Managers. The tendency perhaps was for all-line departments to grow at the expense of the Areas. The civil engineering was taken away from the Areas in 1942 and (despite bitter opposition from all three Divisional General Managers) placed under an all-line Chief Engineer. During the war, moreover, there was sharp criticism from outside of the fragmentation of operating between no less than four Superintendents. It was considered essential that the LNER should have a single representative on the Railway Executive Committee's Operating Sub-committee. So the post of Temporary Assistant General Manager (Operating) was created 'for the duration', its temporary nature being emphasised to mollify the Area Managers.

Some people had mixed feelings about the original LNER organisation. 'It was not a good system for inter-railway matters but for internal matters it was admirable because it provided for the strong local loyalties that continued to exist and were quite healthy.'[51] But some of the 'local loyalties' might be carried to extremes. 'In 1936 . . . I was posted to the Operating department, in fact the timetable department, for the preparation of timetables, and sat in an enormous room with probably thirty or forty other men at their desks. Half the room were GNR men and the other half were GER men, and they were working entirely different systems all for the preparation of timetables. There, on *that* side of the room, they were working with large graphs; here, on *this* side, the Great Eastern men of course said, "Let them have their graphs – they would not work on the Great Eastern – we are much ahead of them" and they were working still on the old dot-and-carry principle.'[52]

If the LNER's decentralisation had its critics, there was also dissatisfaction on the LMS at the extent to which the opposite principle was pushed. 'Centralisation was so great that even the appointment of a stationmaster at a remote rural station, which I recall, on the Carnforth and Settle joint line, was decided at Euston and the chap was sent there by Euston to take up his job.'[53] 'The Midland must have had a tremendous administrative problem in controlling or co-ordinating so many management units direct to headquarters.'[54]

This is a reference to the organisation which the LMS inherited from the Midland Railway, of a large number of District Controllers in charge of operating, reporting direct to a Chief General Superintendent at Derby, a system which lasted until the early 1930s. 'When I got there in 1932 they had only just broken up the tremendous organisation of Chief General Superintendent with his numerous very senior chief officer assistants.'[55]

If the LNER appeared, perhaps only superficially, to be moving towards more centralisation, more all-line departments outside the Area organisation, the LMS, starting from a very different basis, was moving in the opposite direction – towards devolution of power. 'I am told by my old chief at Euston that Lord Stamp's idea, supported by the Vice-Presidents, was to have an organisation of bigger units and a greater jointness of function . . . and to get coterminous boundaries. But Stamp's philosophy as repeated to me . . . was that, in order to reorganise anything, you had to lay it on the table and study it and spread it all out, and then you start drawing it together when you have decided the lines on which you should draw it together.'[56] This seems to have become official policy before nationalisation. 'I am sure it was the intention of the LMS Executive particularly to change the organisation in a major way.'[57]

The main exception to the principle of central control from London on the LMS was the Chief Officer for Scotland. This post had in fact originally been designated Deputy General Manager, Scotland, as a concession to Scottish feeling against control from a remote headquarters in London. Nominally the LMS post carried less direct authority than that of the LNER's Divisional General Manager in Edinburgh.[58] In practice the difference was probably less significant. 'The Scottish end of it was operated not autonomously but with a much greater degree of local independence. It had a home-rule situation . . . I cannot recall any of the hierarchy being much interested in long-distance visits to Scotland or the remoter parts of the empire.'[59]

The Chief Officer for Scotland 'was left, in practice, very much in charge of his own set-up. He did not have a lot of interference. I would not have thought in real terms that his position was very much different from that of the Divisional General Manager of the LNER . . . He had something in the nature of a management committee which included the local chief engineer for Scotland.'[60]

The Southern Railway probably had less difficulty in evolving a satisfactory organisation after grouping than either the LMS or the LNER. It was moreover relatively immune from criticism, whether internal or external, on that particular subject. Certain factors, of course, operated in its favour from the outset. The three main constituent systems radiated south-west, south and south-east from London, and where there was any significant competition – for example, at Portsmouth and (to a smaller extent) at Hastings – this had settled down into working arrangements because joint use of facilities was involved.

In fact, sharing of tracks, whether amicably or otherwise, had been familiar among all the constituent companies of the Southern. The old main line of the South Eastern Railway had until 1868 shared its tracks with the 'Brighton' (in a complicated pattern of ownership) all the way from London Bridge to Redhill; and even after the direct route via Sevenoaks was opened in 1868, certain South Eastern trains for the main line still ran via Redhill, as of course did the trains from the Dover–Ashford–Tonbridge line to Guildford and Reading. Close working between the LBSC and the SECR also existed on the Oxted joint line and the SECR branches to Caterham and Tattenham Corner. Even the peripheral partners in the Southern, the LSWR and the SECR, shared facilities at Guildford and Reading. LSWR trains used SER tracks between Reading and Ash Junction, whilst the SER trains ran over the LSWR from Ash Junction to Shalford Junction.

Accordingly, the Southern's main constituents were neighbours who had long been accustomed to take in some of each other's washing. Once past the first uneasy year of the new grouping it was possible for Sir Herbert Walker, now sole chief executive, to plan the organisation on lines that combined divisional and departmental principles in an effective way.[61] Traffic management was grouped in five Divisions, providing a fair degree of decentralisation. The engineering and other functions were, although administered through geographical subdivisions, more subject to central control. There was an example here (though it was not explicitly expressed) of 'line and staff' principles in the Herbert Walker organisation that seems to have worked well.

The traffic function on the Southern, however, was not decentralised to the same extent as it was on the LNER. 'Up to 1930 there was a Chief Operating Superintendent, a Chief Commercial Manager, and the Divisional Superintendents – you would call them Districts – under them, operating and commercial. In 1930 Walker and Cox set up a Traffic Department and from that there were the Divisional Superintendents only. In the same places but, under them, there was an Operating Assistant and a Commercial Assistant.'[62]

The Southern's Traffic Manager was in a sense the equivalent to the Superintendent of the Line in the traditional railway organisation – in control of operating throughout the system and also of all passenger commercial policy. The main difference was that he also controlled the freight commercial work. The SR Traffic Manager, however, also controlled the Continental Traffic Superintendent, who on the LNER was a chief officer in his own right.

If the Great Western adhered most closely to the traditional departmental pattern, this attracted relatively little criticism from railwaymen outside the Paddington family. 'The Great Western had real qualities and had a unique place in its public character. Yes, they were Victorian in some ways, but there was something special about the Great Western.'[63]

It is worth recalling that the Great Western was about the last company to equip itself with a General Manager in the nineteenth century. C. A. Saunders had been Secretary and General Superintendent (to modern ideas, an odd combination of responsibilities) for many years before he retired in 1863 and James Grierson was made the first General Manager. But even so the independence of the engineering officers was maintained, both the civil and mechanical engineering chiefs having direct access to the Board until J. C. Inglis became General Manager in 1903 and started a long campaign to establish that post as the undoubted chief executive of the railway, a position only finally achieved just before the grouping of 1923.

As the speaker emphasised the 'something special' about the GWR, one may perhaps consider that it may have been partly based upon escaping any need to think very hard about organisation following the grouping. The nearest the GWR got to departing from standard departmental principles was was to create a local co-ordinating position in South Wales, but with much less executive power than the LNER Divisional General Manager in Scotland or even the LMS Chief Officer for Scotland. 'When the war started there was a tremendous amount of traffic going through South Wales and it was at quite an early stage that, with the reduced resources in locomotives particularly, some sort of overriding control was necessary . . . An Assistant to the Superintendent of the Line was appointed in Cardiff who was the operating manager for South Wales. The South Wales Operating Officer with the overriding control quickly became trusted and accepted. We had a very close liaison with the South Wales Coal Owners'Association and kept them very much in the picture.'[64]

The importance of this post seems in fact to have declined once the immediate operating problems faded away. 'After nationalisation the need for that control largely disappeared. On the other hand the South Wales interest, the industrialists, the colliery people, didn't want to go to Paddington with all their questions. The result was that as a sort of compromise the man who had been the sort of Chief Controller for them became the South Wales Area Officer. That worked very well, but apart from being the General Manager's public relations representative he didn't do very much operating then.'[65]

If complacency was sometimes alleged against the Great Western management, the other side of the coin could be put succinctly. 'A more relaxed style reflected a more confident management and confidence was a proven ingredient in the success and effectiveness of Great Western management.'[66]

Organisation had a special significance in those matters in which all the railways were involved, not merely a single company. These were the subject of study and action at two levels – the Railway Companies' Association for matters primarily affecting the interests of the shareholders as represented by the Boards and Chairmen; and the Railway Clearing House for matters that could primarily be regarded as the concern of management. A Clearing House view was that the reduction of 120 companies to four by amalgamation should, *prima facie*, have greatly simplified the Clearing House work in obtaining agreement. But this did not in fact happen. 'Way back in the mid– and late nineteenth century the Clearing House was more of a policy-making body, but from 1914 onwards it was not a policy-making organisation. It made known and acted on policies made by others. We thought that with the amalgamation into four companies the number of committees, and certainly the number of people attending, would fall, whereas in actual fact the numbers grew, very largely because complying with the terms of the 1921 Act involved so much extra committee work. Although you say it is easier to get four companies to agree, the constituents of the four companies still continued to send representatives to Clearing House meetings and whereas, I think, it was the practice – speaking for the commercial side – for the constituents of the main companies to meet before coming to the conference or committee and co-ordinate their views and policies, there were times when even the constituents of the group were not in accord . . . There were disagreements, and Scotland, of course, particularly liked to fly its own flag . . . I thought that the Clearing House secretarial structure, which was based, of course, broadly on the departmental organisation of the railways, was in some respects rather tortuous.'[67]

Whilst the secretarial structure was little simplified, if at all, by the 1923 groupings, the accounting side inevitably diminished as the number of inter-company accounts and the records of junction points diminished. Bagwell has pointed out[68] that the RCH staff had reached a peak of 3,431 employees in March 1922, but this had fallen to about 1,800 by the outbreak of war in 1939.

If the RCH was a large and rather rigid organisation, by comparison the Railway Companies' Association was small and flexible, dealing mainly with parliamentary questions affecting the railways' interests. On occasion the possibility of overlapping was bound to arise. In 1920, for instance, the association was dealing with a subject that might have been considered essentially one for the Clearing House; in that year 'a sub-Committee of the Railway Companies Association ... reached agreement on specification for a 12-ton wagon.'[69]

But later on any such duplication seems to have vanished. 'I do not remember any conflict at all. I think in the early days, of course, when the Companies' Association was formed, there was a certain conflict – in fact, records show that during the first world war there was uncertainty – as to division of function, and there was duplication. But during my office, at any rate, I knew of no conflict at all, except perhaps on the matter of salaries.'[70]

Summing up the division of function, it was said that policy matters, 'such as the general association with the International Union of Railways, were dealt with through the Clearing House. Then, such matters as the adoption of a passenger fare structure and policy of fare reductions to encourage businesses to put their traffic on rail, such as bulk travel, use of bulk travel and traders' tickets, and so on. It was policy, but policy in the narrower sense, not broad policy.' The frontier was quite clearly drawn.[71]

Sherrington, in the study quoted above, considered it to be a strength and not a weakness that no single pattern of organisation had emerged as the best, and that each of the four grouped companies had set about the task in a different manner. The differences were noted by one distinguished outside observer, who felt that the virtues of diversity might be a handicap in a time of emergency. 'It is very important to avoid talking about the four main-line railway companies as though they all acted in the same way. They were very different in their constitution and in the quality of their management and they did not normally act in unison. During the 1939–45 war it was noticeable that the LMS and the LNER adapted very well to the changing traffic circumstances, whereas the Great Western was quite unable to do this. One factor was probably that the Great Western had preserved its identity following the 1921 amalgamations and therefore had been able to preserve its traditional practices unchanged.'[72]

So continuity and tradition might be a source of strength under peacetime or 'normal' conditions; but a handicap in war and 'abnormal' conditions. Nationalisation undoubtedly led to conditions which were 'abnormal' by pre-war standards; and perhaps this explains why organisation patterns that were largely taken for granted between the wars were challenged and changed after 1948.

Notes

1 Railways Act, 1921, s. 3(2)(a).

2 Walker, Sir Herbert Ashcombe, KCB, 1868–1949. Entered LNWR 1885. General Manager, LSWR, 1912. Chairman, Railway Executive Committee, 1913–19. Knighted 1915. General Manager, SR, 1923–37. Director, SR, 1937–47.

3 Granet, Sir (William) Guy, 1867–1943. General Manager, Midland Railway, 1906. Chairman, LMS, 1924–27.

4 Stamp, Lord (Sir Josiah Charles), GCB, GBE, 1880–1941. Entered Inland Revenue 1896. Secretary and Director, Nobel Industries, 1919–26. Director, Imperial Chemical Industries, 1927. Twenty-four doctorates. Numerous presidencies of learned bodies, including Royal Statistical Society. President of the Executive, 1926, Chairman of the Board (also), LMS, 1927.

5 And also for a very short time on the Great Western immediately before nationalisation, when the General Manager, Sir James Milne, was elected to a seat on the Board. The earlier experiences of combining the

posts of Chairman and chief executive – e.g. on the SER and the LCDR – had not been very happy.

6 Royal Commission on Transport, *Final Report* (Cmd. 3751), 1931.

7 Labour Party Report, *The National Planning of Transport*, 1939.

8 A. A. Harrison (LNER).

9 Whitelaw, William, MP (1892–95), 1868–1946. Scottish landowner with industrial interests. Chairman of the Highland, 1902–11, and of the NBR, 1910–22. Chairman, LNER, 1923–38.

10 A. R. Dunbar (LNER).

11 *Ibid.*

12 Wedgwood, Sir Ralph Lewis, CB, CMG, 1874–1956. Knighted 1924: Bt, 1942. Deputy General Manager, NER, 1919–21. General Manager, 1921–22. Chief General Manager, LNER, 1923–39. Chairman, Railway Executive Committee, 1939–41.

13 G. R. Hayes (LNER).

14 *The Railway Interest*, 1973.

15 A. A. Harrison (LNER).

16 A. R. Dunbar (LNER).

17 Matthews, Sir Ronald W., JP, DL, OStJ, 1885–1959. Chairman and Managing Director, Turton Bros. & Matthews, Sheffield. Master Cutler, 1922–23. Director of numerous companies. Chairman, LNER, 1938–47.

18 Newton, Sir Charles H., b. 1882. Assistant Accountant, LNER, 1923. Chief Accountant, LNER, 1928. Divisional General Manager, Southern Area, 1936–39. Chief General Manager, 1939–47.

19 A. R. Dunbar (LNER).

20 Viscount Churchill of Wychwood, GCVO, 1864–1934. Prince of the Holy Roman Empire. Godson of Queen Victoria, Lord Chamberlain at Coronation of King Edward VII. Director of numerous companies. Chairman, GWR, 1908–34.

21 Pole, Sir Felix J. C. 1877–1956, Knighted 1924, General Manager, GWR, 1921–29. Chairman. Associated Electrical Industries, 1929–45.

22 A. W. Tait (GWR).

23 Milne, Sir James, KCVO, CSI, 1883–1958. Knighted 1932. General Manager, GWR, 1929–47.

24 Hambro, Sir Charles, KBE, DL, 1897–1963. Sheriff of County of London, 1933. Banker. Chairman, GWR, 1941.

25 Sir John Elliot (SR).

26 A. W. Tait (GWR).

27 A. A. Harrison (LNER).
28 Sir Felix Pole, *Felix J. C. Pole: his Book*, 1954.
29 Sir John Elliot (SR).
30 *Ibid.*
31 J. L. Harrington (SR).
32 *Ibid.*
33 Sir John Elliot (SR).
34 A. J. Pearson (LMS).
35 *Ibid.*
36 F. Pickstock, *British Railways – the Human Problem* (Fabian Society), 1950, p. 7.
37 P. E. Garbutt (LMS).
38 J. L. Harrington (SR).
39 See, for instance, W. V. Wood and Sir Josiah Stamp, *Railways*, 1928, pp. 137–59; also A. W. Kirkaldy and A. D. Evans, *History and Economics of Transport*, 1915, pp. 195–96.
40 *The Economics of Rail Transport in Great Britain*, 1928, vol. 2, p. 12.
41 *Ibid.*, p. 17.
42 A. W. Tait (GWR).
43 Sherrington, *Economics of Rail Transport*, vol. 2, p. 24.
44 D. S. M. Barrie (LMS).
45 A. R. Dunbar (LNER).
46 *Ibid.*
47 G. F. Fiennes (LNER).
48 A. A. Harrison (LNER).
49 M. A. Cameron (LNER).
50 A. A. Harrison (LNER).
51 G. R. Hayes (LNER).
52 *Ibid.*
53 D. S. M. Barrie (LMS).
54 *Ibid.*
55 *Ibid.*
56 *Ibid.*
57 *Ibid.*
58 Originally titled General Manager (Scotland).
59 P. E. Garbutt (LMS).
60 *Ibid.*
61 C. F. Klapper, *Sir Herbert Walker's Southern Railway*, 1974, p. 93; also M. R. Bonavia, *The Organisation of British Railways*, 1971, p. 28.
62 Sir John Elliot (SR).

63 *Ibid.*
64 A. W. Tait (GWR).
65 *Ibid.*
66 H. H. Phillips (GWR).
67 T. J. Lynch (RCH).
68 P. S. Bagwell, *The Railway Clearing House in the British Economy, 1842–1922*, 1968, p. 282.
69 P. S. Bagwell, *The Transport Revolution from 1770*, 1974, p. 238.
70 T. J. Lynch (RCH). 'The matter of salaries' relates to an objection by the General Managers to salaries for staff of the Association being fixed without reference to comparable salaries within the companies.
71 T. J. Lynch (RCH).
72 A. Bull (LT).

2

The quality of management

It has often been remarked[1] that the railways' principles of staffing and discipline have much in common with those of the armed forces. The 'officers and other ranks' of the army were in the past closely parallelled by the 'officers and servants' of the company. (In fact the term 'railway servant' has only dropped out of use comparatively recently.) Luncheon rooms provided for railway managers are still 'messes'; references to 'brother officers' are not considered out of place.

This sense of separation from the non-railway (or even the 'civilian') world leads to an outlook that still differs significantly from that in the general sphere of industry. Undoubtedly the fact that railway safety, in the days before mechanical and electrical safeguards had been devised, depended almost entirely upon the discipline exercised by railwaymen was significant in developing virtually a Service mentality. 'It is cloistered in this business . . . basically a railway works on its rules and regulations, so you have people who are trained to work on basic rules and regulations, and the vital element in that is safety.'[2]

In other words, special standards are claimed. Yet throughout the period of this study the railway Boards were, or should have been, motivated by ordinary commercial considerations in so far as they were responsible to their shareholders for maximising profits within the limits set by the Railways Act, 1921. Were the managers they employed competent in the pursuit of this objective? What was the outside view of their performance?

There are not very many recorded criticisms of the quality of railway management, as distinct from criticisms of the quality of railway policy. The Labour Party and the three major railway trade unions, committed as they were in principle to nationalisation of the railways, criticised the system of private ownership and the existence of Boards of Directors. But there are few attacks on management itself, apart from the policies it was required to follow. There was one exception to this during the House of Commons debate on railway nationalisation on 17 November 1937, when a Labour MP, J. Henderson, was reported in the press to have referred to 'a redundancy of very highly paid officials'. In reply to this a booklet published by *Modern Transport* but obviously inspired by the railways,[3] pointed out that in 1936 total monthly salaries (i.e. clerical as well as managerial staff costs) amounted to only about 0·7 per cent of total receipts – a very low proportion in comparision with most businesses.

The relations between senior trade union negotiators and their opposite numbers on the management side of the table were generally quite good, and the sharpness with which union cases were argued was not accompanied as a rule by any specific criticism of individuals on the other side. Negotiation was in fact a kind of chess match in which personal hostility did not usually enter: the rules of the game were well understood.

A former trade union official commented upon the effectiveness of the manager class in the late 1920s and early 1930s: 'Whilst there is no doubt that they [then] had more power and could exercise more fear over people, I think they were efficient.'[4]

Boards and, by implication, their managements were, however, accustomed to be criticised, sometimes keenly, by shareholders at annual general meetings. Of course, only a tiny proportion of the railway shareholders, who numbered over a million, troubled to turn up, and they were often those with a grievance or a suggestion to make. But criticisms were often directed to minor matters and normally the Chairman would have little difficulty in finding either a refutation or an appeasing reply. There is not much evidence that points urged by shareholders on these occasions were effective in influencing policy in the inter-war period. Certain shareholders were known to be perennial critics – for example, a certain Councillor Wilson regularly harangued the LMS and LNER general meetings, year after year, and on occasion had to be peremptorily directed by the Chairman to resume his seat. But even Councillor Wilson did not attack the managers of the least financially successful main-line railway – only the Board of the LNER.

It may be therefore concluded that the efficiency or otherwise of individual managers was assessed internally, and their promotion adjusted accordingly, by standards that the outside world was scarcely able to evaluate. The public appearances of the most senior managers – men such as Stamp, Wedgwood, Milne and Walker – before any tribunal or body of enquiry certainly gave an impression of total mastery of the subject under examination. These were public figures, able to hold their own anywhere. This impression of the potentates of the railway service is, broadly, echoed by those who have compiled railway histories. C. Hamilton Ellis has written that 'Sir Josiah Stamp was . . . a puritan, and one with a Civil Service training at that, but he was a man of fresh ideas and very formidable intellect'.[5] The list of Stamp's non-railway distinctions is impressive; it includes being president (1931–32) of the Royal Statistical Society; director of Imperial Chemical Industries; British representative on the Reparations Commission Committee on German currency and finance; CBE in 1918, KBE in 1920 and GBE in 1924.

An internal view of him was that 'he was silver-tongued: he could appear before a Royal Commission and put his case magnificently. He could appear on the Square Deal Committee or campaign. He could go to Parliament; he could go where he liked. At the same time, he was advising people like MacDonald, then the Prime Minister. Even when he was killed in the war, all government papers were in his house and had to be found. He was an adviser to the government in all sorts of ways. He was a great co-ordinator.'[6]

Stamp had been briefly preceded by two General Managers of the LMS, Sir Arthur Watson[7] and the Rt Hon. H. G. Burgess,[8] whose tenure in each case was less than a couple of years and need not be enlarged upon. Stamp's death in an air raid on 16 April 1941 led to the unforeseen succession to the LMS presidency (though not the chairmanship) of Sir William V. Wood,[9] the senior Vice-President. Wood had been a splendid back-room supporter of Stamp, but he was not a public figure of the same calibre. 'Stamp had Wood there who could produce anything, any figure you liked he could find. And they were accurate; I mean, they would stand in a court of law as evidence and he was a witness many, many times. But he was inarticulate . . . he had a very, very bad Irish brogue and he used to stick a cigarette in and make the brogue fifty times worse. His handwriting was also very difficult. The result was that nobody knew what Wood said and nobody knew what Wood wrote. When I arrived there, I became the interpreter of Wood and when anybody came to see Wood, they also came to see me and then, of course, I took them into Wood and they did not know what was said so I told them what was said. That is how Wood became intelligible. So you had a gifted man who was a Vice-President when I first knew him and people thought he was very bright although they could not understand him.'[10]

Of Sir Ralph Wedgwood a character sketch by Cecil J. Allen supports the external impression he created of an outstanding railway manager: 'Sir Ralph was the embodiment of the classical quality *gravitas*, and, certainly to the younger elements, a somewhat awe-inspiring figure . . . the awe owed much . . . to the intellectual power which Wedgwood brought to bear on every item reaching his desk, and the lucidity with which his views and judgements were expressed. His letters on major subjects, and his policy directives, were couched in language which had all the force and authority of Papal encyclicals . . . But . . . it must not be thought that Wedgwood ever ceased to be a railwayman to the core . . . he was able to appreciate every detail of the proposals and plans put before him by his officers . . . His great gifts showed at their best when he was in the witness-box.'[11]

An impression of remoteness from the rough-and-tumble of management could be attributed partly to the LNER organisation under which day-to-day running of the railways was entrusted to three Divisional General Managers and effectively controlled by the Chief General Manager only on company policy matters; partly to Wedgwood's own temperament. As Allen remarks, 'smoking concerts and similar "get-togethers" were not altogether in his line of country'.

Wedgwood's remoteness, his intellectuality, and perhaps his ability to see both sides of a question, seem in later years to have impaired his effectiveness. His remoteness had always been felt. 'Only once that I can recall did I meet him when he was out on tour with the Board and passed my territory; whereas Bell[12] we knew and the other headquarters people we knew.'[13]

Later, when Wedgwood was perhaps past his most effective period, criticism of his lack of decisiveness grew. 'I have found a note among my papers that Ralph Wedgwood was found particularly difficult. He seemed to have great trouble in making up his mind. I have a note to suggest that there were occasions when Herbert Walker – the Southern Railway had a much greater interest in the pooling scheme than the LNER – would have come to a solution but Wedgwood perhaps deferred and delayed for further consideration. He referred it back to the accountants – that kind of thing. I don't say that he discouraged debate. I think his difficulty always was in taking decisions. He was a very careful man, careful perhaps because of the financial difficulties of his railway.'[14]

There seems to have been general agreement that Sir Charles Newton, who succeeded him as Chief General Manager in 1938, although a sincere and likable personality, was not of the same intellectual stature. His relationship with Sir Ronald Matthews has already been mentioned (page 00): and in any case the war broke out so soon after his appointment that his scope for innovation was very limited.

The Great Western had two General Managers during the period – Sir Felix Pole (1923–29) and Sir James Milne (1929–47). Both were career railwaymen, brought up in the Great Western 'family' tradition; but they seem to have been very different characters, though both strong in their way. On Pole it was commented, 'Every little bit that you'd done, he expected to cross-examine you on. Life was hard, as you can imagine. Pole was succeeded by Milne and during the first few weeks I said to Milne, "Do you want me to carry through the same procedure so far as the Clearing House minutes are concerned?" He said, "Not ruddy likely. I don't keep a dog and bark myself. You tell me the ones I ought to know something about." A complete difference. But it meant that there was more responsibility on my shoulders.'[15]

Two different management styles at the top level! Pole had had problems of control over departmental chiefs. 'Now it was the rule, or tradition, that the Accountant had direct access to the Board, not through the General Manager. Pole always felt that that was wrong because he felt that if the General Manager was responsible through his other Chief Officers for authorising expenditure and that sort of thing, he also should have some control over the Accountants. So that it is true that there was a friction between them.'[16]

Pole seems to have been a perfectionist and to have perhaps lacked the skill to steer a team of individualist departmental heads, thus provoking a measure of hostility that left him isolated when he clashed with his Chairman, Viscount Churchill. Milne, though also a strong personality, seems to have assessed more realistically the strength of his own position, particularly in relation to his directors, with the result that he was elected to the GWR Board in 1947, whilst remaining General Manager – an honour which the Ministry of Transport would not allow him to take up, on the ground that as a member of the Railway Executive Committee under government control he could not also represent the shareholders' interests.

Of the Southern's General Manager from 1923 until 1937, it is hard to find any written reference that is not eulogistic. Walker's regime was successful mainly owing to his capacity for leadership, which has been eloquently described by more than one of his former subordinates. 'He was one of the finest leaders not merely of railwaymen but . . . a natural leader who inspired confidence . . . Walker had such a good team because he was a wonderful captain . . . [He] was pre-eminently a quiet man . . . no decision of major importance was taken without [his] approval and, more often than not, was at his original instigation . . . Walker was a wonderfully good example of the intelligent and professional general manager.'[17] 'I feel that Walker was something by himself . . . which is rather strange, I think, for a run-of-the-mill railman, a great financier.'[18] Walker could even be compared, not to his disadvantage, with Stamp. 'Elizabeth [Harrington], who knew Stamp and danced with him on occasions, still insists to this day that *Walker* was the most impressive man she ever met.'[19]

Walker's stature had already been recognised by his election to a directorship of the Southern upon his retirement from the general managership. One breath of mild criticism can be found. 'If Walker had a fault it was the lack of small talk, the shy restraint that held him from conviviality.' But even this was mitigated by his assiduous learning of 'the names of all grades from porters to drivers with whom he was likely to come into contact on outdoor expeditions . . . by this . . . he was always able to make men feel at home with their General Manager.'[20] His other weakness, of which he became well aware, was a lack of appreciation of the place of public relations in a service industry – a fault which he corrected most effectively in due course (p. 000 below).

His successor, G. S. Szlumper,[21] was a very different character – genial, outgoing and outspoken. He was not in office long enough to make a major individual contribution to policy development, which would in any case have been difficult in view of the great impetus imparted by Walker and the Walker imprint upon the whole managerial organisation.

One can perhaps sum up by saying that the individual chief executives of the railways during the greater part of the period seem all to have been regarded, by general consent, as men of outstanding ability although of different temperaments and with individual managerial techniques. It was in the middle and lower ranks that the quality of management was more open to question. A. J. Pearson, himself a former very senior railway officer, wrote that the system 'makes for inbreeding and a conservative outlook'.[22] Aldcroft refers to 'the possibility that the leaders of the industry will maintain a continued faith in old techniques and distrust the new, with which they are not familiar'.[23] He suggests that 'the failure to recruit managerial staff from outside the profession . . . meant that the prospects for questioning traditional railway practice were limited'.[24]

If judgements on the quality of individual managers within their own company are lacking (apart from the implied judgements contained in the course of their careers), a fairly impartial external view of managers in action could be obtained by the Railway Clearing House, where the secretarial side (as distinct from the accounting side) was responsible for organising meetings of officers, from General Managers down through departmental heads, assistant departmental heads, to departmental representatives, to consider and try to reach decisions upon a vast range of subjects in which more than one company was involved. A clearly expressed view was that at the top level: 'when the General Managers had before them the minutes of the departmental committee, they made decisions straight away. Only rarely did they refer something back.'[25] On the other hand, such effectiveness was often lacking lower down. 'The chief officers . . . if there was not immediate agreement . . . would refer it to the assistants, and quite often the assistants after discussion would then refer it to the lower committee, the representatives. It would then go back to the assistants and from the assistants back to the chiefs . . . that could take perhaps a couple of months . . . there was a lack of urgency to answer questions.'[26] The Clearing House representative at such meetings was supposed merely to act as a note-taker, and on occasion this could be frustrating. 'There are times when the secretary gets a little tired of squabbles with people who will sidetrack the main discussion and the secretary is left to pick out the pieces that matter . . . he dare not intervene.'[27]

The impression is left of a body of railway managers by no means immune from the faults of administrators in every walk of life: where the sting of competition is not sharply felt, the pressure to act swiftly and decisively is lacking.

There were, however, exceptions to the general in-breeding. 'Although some people thought that the LMS were reluctant to take in outside talent . . . this was not the case in the advertising department at Euston . . . eventually most of the production work in the department was being done by people who had come in from outside.'[28] The LMS certainly imported a number of people at high levels, quite apart from the advertising side. Sir Harold Hartley[29] became a Vice-President direct from outside. An American office efficiency expert was appointed to set up an Executive Research Office to rationalise the paper work within the company. A soldier, Brigadier Manton,[30] was recruited as Principal of the LMS School of Transport at Derby.

In other companies it is difficult to find similar examples of the infusion of new blood from outside, apart from the outstanding case of J. B. Elliot, later Sir John Elliot,[31] who was recruited to the Southern Railway (from being Assistant Editor of the *Evening Standard*) to become Public Relations Assistant to the General Manager, Sir Herbert Walker, in 1925.

Apart from generalisations about the quality of railway managers over the period, it is relevant to consider whether there were any significant variations as between the four railways. Here one should probably seek an outside view, since company loyalty seems often to colour the comments of those who served a main-line railway. 'The London & North Eastern Railway Company seemed to me to be outstanding in one way only, and that was in the recruitment, education and training programmes introduced by Robert Bell[32] as Assistant General Manager, for bringing in well qualified graduates and training them in railway management. These graduates afterwards provided something like 50 per cent of the technical officers in the Transportation and Movement Divisions of the British army during the second world war, and they provided very nearly 50 per cent of the senior management of British Railways during the days of the British Transport Commission, 1948 onwards . . . the interesting point is whether this large group of very able young men . . . if the war had not occurred, would have succeeded in transforming the position of the LNER and bringing it up to or perhaps surpassing the standards which were being set at that time by the Southern Railway and the London Midland & Scottish Railway.'[33]

The LNER was of course not the only company to recruit in this way, but it was the only one to recruit so systematically and on such a scale. 'The London Midland & Scottish Railway . . . recruited engineers, technicians, economists. They do not seem to have seen the same need for highly trained minds in traffic operation . . . they had a small number of traffic apprentices . . . the Great Western had a small number of traffic apprentices . . . the Southern had a small number of traffic apprentices . . . but the LNER did very much more than the other undertakings.'[34]

The predominance of former LNER traffic apprentices in BR in the early years after nationalisation had been parallelled earlier on, at the grouping, within the LNER itself. The fact that the North Eastern Railway had pioneered and extended the traffic apprenticeship scheme meant that within the group the influence of former North Eastern men was disproportionately strong.

Rather different reasons had led to a similar imbalance of management weighting within the LMS after the grouping, as a former officer of that company recalled. 'The LNWR was a very "gentlemanly" railway. When the 1914–18 war broke out a very high proportion of its younger managers and "cadets" volunteered for service in HM forces – far more than on the Midland or on the L&Y. This had its effect in the immediate post-war and grouping period, when the stay-at-homes tended to have reached senior positions and outnumbered the others.'

One is bound to ask whether a system of management development operated by one man, such as that of Bell on the LNER, did not lead to favouritism and misjudgement on occasion. Few from the LNER agreed with this. 'He certainly had an enormous range of knowledge of us all. We never knew how he got it. If you went to see him, there was that enormous head just above the desk and he would suddenly flatten you . . . Robert Bell was dry and Scots and as a rule took you down a peg or two. I think he sorted the sheep from the goats pretty well . . . if he said of anybody that he was "clerkly" that chap was finished, almost without exception.'[36] 'It was a personal triumph, in a sense, for Robert Bell that this system worked as well as it did.'[37] A slightly more critical view of the 'Bell empire' argued that 'It wasn't a good thing, but it perhaps suited the circumstances of the time. It was certainly accepted. People didn't seem to resent it. Of course, where he derived his power was in his control of the traffic apprentice scheme . . . He used to see these chaps once every six months or every year . . . the little black book which he kept in his desk . . . He ran the top salaried section very much himself with that kind of help. But . . . he was always at pains to be constitutional. In other words, he always worked through the machine, through the Divisional Managers, and although effectively the decisions were his – Robert Bell's – he never sidestepped the machine. He was punctilious in ways of that sort, and that was perhaps partly where his strength lay, and of course in his personality, but primarily in the tight control he kept on the traffic apprenticeship scheme.'[38]

Criticism of the traffic apprenticeship schemes is not very common, but Joy has argued that 'whilst [the scheme] makes for eminently capable operating managers, it has definite disadvantages at the highest levels, where memories of Whitemoor yard, Bradford Valley goods depot or Crewe works impose an unnecessary brake on thoughts of grand strategy . . . On the way up, especially in the inter-war years, men were plentiful but equipment was old and scarce. Hence the fetish, once in power, for solving yesterday's problems.'[39]

Whether this criticism is valid or not, it should be mentioned that quite a number of former LNER traffic apprentices left the railway to find successful careers in business, in which their railway training seems to have stood them in good stead.[40] One can only conjecture how far the quality of management would have been strengthened had they remained with the railway. But LNER salaries were low by comparison with those in the other companies. 'The LNE grading salary scales were miles below those of the others. My father told me that as Assistant to Passenger Manager for passenger rates and fares he was getting about £500 a year and his counterpart on the LMS . . . was then getting nearer £1,000. Father only had the Southern Area, a smaller empire, but all the way down it was the same. At the station I was at, Welwyn Garden City, there were five clerks, all Grade 5, the lowest. The LMS would have had a Grade 3 chief clerk, two Grade 4s and three 5s. It was all the way down pared to the bone.'[41]

High thinking on the LNER was certainly accompanied by plain living! In the league table, although salaries remained nominally confidential, it was generally accepted that, if the LNER came at the bottom, the LMS came at the top. This also applied to the salaried staff superannuation scheme on the LMS, whose benefits were the best of those in the four companies.

Whilst it may be generally true that in the last analysis the quality of management can only be tested by the results it is seen to have produced – and these will be examined in subsequent chapters – nevertheless there are two remaining questions for consideration. These are the extent, if any, to which nepotism was practised; and the extent, if any, to which management development was consciously and effectively carried out.

Railways have almost always been of a size that transcended any idea of family control. Even the Pease dynasty did not treat the Stockton & Darlington, or the North Eastern, as a fief in the age of patronage. Only a few small railways have in the past been utterly dominated by a single personality such as Lundie[42] of the Rhymney Railway.

Originally recruits to the clerical staff had needed to obtain nomination by a director, but this soon became obsolete as railways developed into large bureaucracies. Favouritism there may have been, but specific nepotism was rather rare. Sir Edward Watkin[43] was certainly guilty of it when he appointed his son, who was unsuitable for the post, as Locomotive Superintendent of the SER – an appointment which the Board overturned within a year. But such episodes have been exceptional, and preceded the period now under study. Cecil Paget,[44] the dynamic General Superintendent of the Midland Railway, had been the son of a Chairman of the company. Some Chief Mechanical Engineers were succeeded by their sons[45] but real talent often ran in families, as did loyalty to the railway service.[46]

In fact right up to the present day family connection has been a regular source of recruitment. Second, third and even fourth-generation railwaymen exist; recruitment to the female staff, mainly clerks and typists, has commonly been from the daughters, sisters and nieces of railwaymen.

One retired senior officer explained that 'my father was with the old Great Northern and LNER as Assistant to Passenger Manager, Southern Area. My paternal grandfather was one of the senior foremen in Doncaster carriage works, having started on the old Great Northern in the old carriage shops at Kings Cross in the 1860s. Again, a great-uncle was Carriage and Wagon Inspector on the Manchester Sheffield & Lincolnshire Railway at Barnetby, and on the maternal side my grandmother's own cousin retired as Assistant to the Accountant, Southern Area, of the LNER, after having been Audit Accountant of the old Great Northern Railway.'[47]

But the officer in question was *not* given a flying start on account of his family background. 'I graduated at LSE in 1928 with the BCom degree, my special subject being inland transport. Then the LNER rejected me as a TA on the grounds that I was too immature, but Mr Bell said that if I was prepared to join as a Grade 5 clerk and could prove I had the ability and the will to work I would have a reasonable chance of making good.'[48]

On the Great Western, where there were also management training schemes, one comment was: 'There were, it is true, fewer management trainees than in the LNER. Promotion, for the generality, tended to be by seniority. But I think in all departments – this was borne out by my own experience – the heads of the departments were very keen indeed on spotting talent and bringing forward certain individuals fairly rapidly. It was the policy of the company to appoint officers relatively young. Pole was General Manager at just over forty. Dashwood[49] would have been Chief Accountant at forty if his predecessor had not stayed on until he was seventy-five!'[50]

The total spectrum of management development now covers initial training, vocational training, career planning, job rotation and management succession. This formal pattern is largely a post-nationalisation development, since recruitment to managerial posts in the period under study was mainly by promotion from the clerical grades. Those grades (Classes 1–5 plus Special Class) were filled by school leavers entering in the 'starting grade', Class 5, or perhaps as a temporary clerk awaiting entry to the permanent staff, and moving upwards by a combination of seniority and merit towards the dizzy height of Special Class, which the majority never attained before retirement overtook them.

Within this rather rigid system there were two 'escape routes'. One was the educational facilities provided, or assisted financially, by the companies for staff who were anxious to fit themselves for promotion.

The educational facilities in all companies included evening classes in subjects such as station working, passenger and goods station accounts, operating principles, and so on. The LNER was in the lead (at any rate until the LMS established a well equipped residential School of Transport at Derby) with its two residential establishments, the All-Line Commercial School at Faverdale and the All-Line Operating School at Darlington, both rather appropriately situated in the nursery of railways, the North Eastern Area. Later the Southern Railway opened a similar establishment at Woking in the building which in 1959, after nationalisation, became the British Transport Staff College.

The second 'escape route' was of course the special training schemes – on the LNER the Traffic Apprenticeships, on the Southern the Cadetships, for example – which have already been discussed on pp. 000 000.

It can hardly be said, therefore, that the railways lagged behind industry in general in management development through training. During the 1920s and 1930s it certainly seems that they preserved and improved the quality of their management by using such techniques and practices as were available.

Notes

1 See, for instance, S. Joy, *The Train that Ran Away*, 1973, p. 33.
2 A. J. Pearson (LMS).
3 *The Nationalization of Transport: an Impartial Review*, June 1938, p. 36. The authorship was anonymous but Sir Josiah Stamp contributed a foreword.
4 D. Robertson (Railway Clerks' Association).
5 C. Hamilton Ellis, *London Midland and Scottish*, 1970, p. 98.
6 A. J. Pearson (LMS).
7 Sir Arthur Watson, CBE, 1873–1954. Superintendent of the Line, LYR, General Manager, LYR (1919–20). General Manager, LNWR, 1921–23. General Manager, LMS, 1923–24.
8 Rt. Hon. H. Givens Burgess, PC (Ireland, 1922), 1859–1937. Scottish representative and later Irish Traffic Manager, LNWR. General Manager, LMS, 1924–27.
9 Sir William Valentine Wood, KBE, 1883–1959. Controller of Costs

and Statistics, LMS, 1927. Vice-President (Finance and Services), 1930. President of the Executive, 1941–47. Member, British Transport Commission, 1947–53.

10 A. J. Pearson (LMS).

11 Cecil J. Allen, *The London and North Eastern Railway*, 1971, p. 59.

12 Robert Bell, CBE, 1877–1966. Joined NER, 1898. Assistant Goods Manager, then (1922) Assistant General Manager, NER. Assistant General Manager, LNER, 1923. Retired 1943.

13 A. R. Dunbar (LNER).

14 A. Bull (LT).

15 H. H. Phillips (GWR).

16 *Ibid.*

17 Sir John Elliot (SR).

18 J. L. Harrington (SR).

19 *Ibid.*

20 C. F. Klapper, *Sir Herbert Walker's Southern Railway*, 1974, p. 12.

21 Major-General Gilbert S. Szlumper, CBE, TD, 1884–1969. Assistant to General Manager LSWR, 1913. Secretary to Railway Executive Committee, 1914–19. Assistant General Manager, SR, 1925–37. General Manager, SR, 1937–42. Director General of Transportation and Movements, War Office, 1939–40.

22 A. J. Pearson, *The Railways and the Nation*, 1964, p. 31.

23 D. H. Aldcroft, *Studies in British Transport History, 1870–1970*, 1974, p. 247.

24 D. H. Aldcroft, *British Transport since 1914*, 1975, p. 254.

25 T. J. Lynch (RCH).

26 *Ibid.*

27 *Ibid.*

28 D. S. M. Barrie (LMS).

29 Brigadier-General Sir Harold Hartley, GCVO, CH, CBE, FRS, MC, 1878–1972. Chairman, Fuel Research Board. Fellow of Balliol College, Oxford. Vice-President (Research), LMS, 1932. Chairman, Railway Air Services, 1934. Left LMS 1945: Chairman, British European Airways, 1946; Chairman, British Overseas Airways Corporation, 1947.

30 Brigadier L. Manton, OBE, DSO, b. 1887. Assistant Director of Transportation, British Troops in Egypt, 1935–36. Principal, LMS School of Transport, Derby, 1936–39. Director of Transportation, India, 1941–42. Principal, British Railways School of Transport, Derby, 1947–51.

31 Elliot, Sir John (Kt. 1954), b. 1898. Assistant Editor, *Evening Standard*, 1924–25. Public Relations Assistant to General Manager, SR, 1925. Assistant General Manager, SR, 1937. General Manager, 1947. Chief Regional Officer, Southern Region, 1948–49, London Midland Region, 1950–51. Chairman, Railway Executive, 1951–53. Chairman, London Transport Executive, 1953–59.

32 Strictly, the former NER programmes, which Bell extended to the rest of the LNER system.

33 A. Bull (LT).

34 *Ibid.*

35 P. J. Fisher (LMS).

36 G. F. Fiennes (LNER).

37 M. A. Cameron (LNER).

38 G. R. Hayes (LNER).

39 Joy, *The Train that Ran Away*, pp. 33–4.

40 E.g. C. A. Lambert (former Passenger Manager, North Eastern Area) became General Manager, Bolsover Colliery Co.; W. M. Teasdale (former Assistant General Manager) became Head of Advertising, Allied Newspapers; F. C. C. Stanley (former District Passenger Manager, Newcastle) became Managing Director, B&N Line.

41 C. E. Whitworth (Railway Research Service).

42 Cornelius Lundie, 1815–1908. Entered railway service in north-eastern England and became Traffic Manager, Blyth & Tyne Railway. Traffic Manager, Rhymney Railway, 1862: later General Manager until 1904. Director, Rhymney Railway, 1904.

43 Sir Edward William Watkin, 1819–1901. Secretary, Trent Valley Railway, 1845. General Manager, MSLR, 1853. President, Grand Trunk Railway (Canada), 1861. Chairman, MSLR, 1864. Chairman, SER, 1866–94. Chairman, Metropolitan Railway, 1872–94. Director, GWR, 1866; GER, 1867. Chairman, Channel Tunnel Co., 1872.

44 Paget, Lieutenant-Colonel Sir Cecil Walter (Bt.), CMG, DSO, 1874–1936. Son of Sir (George) Ernest Paget, Bt. General Superintendent, MR. Resigned to enter industry.

45 E.g. T. W. Worsdell and Wilson Worsdell (NER); James Holden and Stephen Dewar Holden (GER); T. Whitelegg and R. H. Whitelegg (LTSR); R. J. Billinton and L. B. Billinton (LBSCR); J. Beattie and W. G. Beattie (LSWR). Less significant are the posts on different railways held by brothers (e.g. Dugald and Peter Drummond, Patrick and James Stirling) or by uncle and nephew (Matthew and William Kirtley).

46 A rider to this was: 'There was nepotism on the LNWR . . . I would cite the Kinsman and the Williams families and there were others. It was specifically frowned upon by the NER.' (A. A. Harrison, LNER.)

47 C. E. Whitworth (Railway Research Service).

48 *Ibid.*

49 C. R. Dashwood, CBE, 1888–1962. Assistant Accountant, GWR, 1923. Assistant General Manager, GWR, 1934. Chief Accountant, GWR, 1938. Chairman of the Accountants Committees of the Railway Companies' Association and Railway Executive Committee, 1940. Chief Accountant, Western Region, BR, 1948–53.

50 A. W. Tait (GWR).

3

Labour costs, productivity and staff morale

Various writers, perhaps relying rather heavily upon hindsight, have suggested that the railways were slow to adopt new methods between the wars, and that this, by implication, affected the efficiency with which they used their labour force. Aldcroft, for instance, writes, 'Freight handling methods remained grossly inefficient . . . railway wagons were too small,[1] too lightly loaded and badly marshalled . . . the scope for further economies by rationalising services and pruning the uneconomic parts of the system was enormous but neither course of action was seriously contemplated by the railways in this period.'[2] The same writer comments elsewhere that 'reaction to the new techniques tended . . . to be defensive . . . the prospects for questioning traditional railway practice were limited'.[3]

To test these assertions is not easy. One comment is very relevant. 'There were not the positive measurements of labour productivity that have been available since the 1939–45 war.'[4]

Even since the war, D. L. Munby's study of British railways' productivity was hampered by the fact that, as he pointed out, 'neither a passenger mile nor a ton mile is a homogeneous unit of output'.[5] Crude statistics, such as traffic units (ton miles of freight plus passenger miles) per unit of total staff employed, may give a very rough indication of trends in a single undertaking over a period of time; but they are quite unreliable as an indicator of relative labour productivity on *different* railway systems, owing to operating practices and the different extent to which tasks are carried out by the railway staff or by contractors – e.g.

permanent way maintenance.

Munby was able to draw some broad conclusions over the period 1938 to 1960 by measuring changes in wagon utilisation, work performed by locomotives, and output per worker. But applying his method to the years 1923 to 1937 is less easy because passenger-mile statistics were not compiled for the period. However, net ton miles and originating passengers provide separate if not entirely satisfactory indices which may be compared with the index of staff numbers, as in the accompanying table, for the four main-line railways.

The figures are given for 1923, the first year after grouping; for 1929, when the 'economies of scale' (if any) should have taken effect, but before the depression; for 1933, in the trough of the depression; and for 1937, when recovery had taken place, but before the 'mini-recession' of 1938.

Table 2
Staff, passengers and net ton miles on the railways, 1923–37

	1923	*1929*	*1933*	*1937*
Staff numbers (000)	651	613	539	575
Index	100	94	83	88
Originating passengers (million)	877	815	748	847
Index	100	93	85	97
Net ton miles (million)	18,485	18,375	14,640	17,935
Index	100	99	79	97

These figures certainly suggest a modest productivity improvement by 1937, the passenger and freight indices in that year each showing 97 per cent of the 1923 figures, contrasting with a staff of just under 88 per cent of the 1923 figure.

A rather more useful result can be obtained by comparing, in selected grades, the numbers employed with the relevant output. Thus numbers of footplate staff and guards can be compared with train and engine hours, and train and engine mileage.

The total train miles in 1937 were 421·2 million, compared with 368·8 million in 1923, an increase of 14 per cent, largely due to the need for more frequent services rather than growth in traffic.

Drivers (and motormen of electric trains) concerned with operating passenger and freight trains in fact fell over the period by 2 per cent. Firemen (and assistant motormen) fell by 10 per cent. Signalmen (and signal box lads) fell by 13 per cent, partly owing to signalling concentration schemes; and shunters by 6 per cent. Staff concerned solely with passenger train operation, i.e. passenger guards, fell by 7 per cent against an increase (chiefly on the Southern Railway) in passenger train mileage of 23 per cent. Goods guards fell by 13 per cent, against a drop of 3½ per cent in goods train mileage. Engine cleaners fell by 50 per cent, in part reflecting the reduction in the total number of steam locomotives from 23,879 to 19,679, or 17½ per cent; in part probably owing to a lower standard of cleaning, and perhaps also to difficulty, in some industrial areas, in recruiting staff for this class of heavy work after the worst of the depression had passed.

Within the total for the four main lines, the Southern Railway figures are particularly interesting, since that railway showed an overall increase in passenger-train miles of 50 per cent – from 41·1 million to 61·7 million between 1923 and 1937 – substantially more than the national increase. Whilst in 1923 only 5·1 million miles had been with electric traction, in 1937 the SR figure was 33·1 million or 54 per cent of the total. In consequence, the number of Southern drivers and motormen rose, but only very slightly, from 3,595 in 1923 to 3,849 in 1937, by no more than one per cent; whilst firemen and assistant motormen fell from 3,740 to 2,960, a reduction of 11 per cent. The improvement in labour productivity from electrification is obvious.

The LMS was particularly energetic in its search for economies, shown by the drastic overhaul of workshop practices, the 'cyclic diagramming' of locomotive turns of duty and the creation of an Executive Research Office to standardise forms and documents throughout the organisation.

The company sponsored a special supplement to *The Economist* dated 31 August 1938 in which the management's achievements and problems were reviewed. On labour productivity, the survey stressed that 'it has never been practicable to distinguish amalgamation economies from those due to technical progress. For example, more adequate lubricating apparatus and improved locomotive design produce fuel economy and a longer annual engine mileage; and such economies will continue, year after year. Developments like the installation of automatic signals, a modern hotel, mechanical carriage cleaning, spray painting, all-electric signals cabins, a new steamer, a reconstructed station – like that obtained by the combination of Leeds (Wellington) and Leeds (New) into Leeds City – all these reduce the demand for labour, and labour reputedly accounts for over 60 per cent of railway working costs.'

The article went on to emphasise the limitations that existed at that time upon the management's power to effect economies from greater labour productivity. It continued: 'Labour costs, in theory variable, have since the war been relatively rigid. All the British railways have complex agreements with their staffs for a guaranteed week and a guaranteed day. Their inability to lay off permanent staff temporarily has been a social advantage, but a stockholder's disability. Against a fall of 12 per cent in receipts in nine years, the maximum reduction in staff wages and salaries rates was 5 per cent.'

This contemporary comment may be set against the argument of subsequent writers, such as Aldcroft, that the limitations upon improving labour productivity in the 1920s and 1930s were due to an inadequate effort on the part of management. The recorded comments by 'insiders' upon this point are quite emphatic. 'You are looking at it with hindsight. And you had not got all the methods that you have now. There were no such things as computers and equipment like that to quicken everything. They had to go through the laborious job of all your work with manual labour. Now you do it with electronic devices. It is a totally different world.'[6]

Another comment was: 'Productivity is, after all, a modern connotation which we wouldn't have understood in those years. In those days, you had a certain number of signal boxes and they had to be manned for twenty-four hours, sixteen hours a day or whatever it was, and you didn't look beyond that, as long as you could cover your duties on those signal boxes. We didn't think about abolishing signal boxes or only having one signal box between King's Cross and Peterborough. We hadn't got to that technical age.'[7]

This point was emphasised in another way. 'On the freight side, some of the things which came out in the 1950s might have been thought of in the 1930s. Containerisation – horrible word: the LMS made a start with it but really didn't press it very far, and the LNE sort of picked at it. Merry-go-round – the principle of discharging from hopper wagons on to conveyor belts in a hole in the ground – as simple as that – and loading from overhead bunkers, coal, ores, and that sort of thing. I don't see why that shouldn't have been thought of in the 1930s except that we didn't think of it. Full train-load working – it took the war to teach us the advantages of that. All of those things could have been done.

'But, having said that, of course the companies did a very great deal. When I went to Whitemoor as assistant yard master in 1931, all the traffics out of East Anglia – and there was a very great deal of it, not only Continental through Harwich – all the vegetables and the fruit, and the industrial products of north London, Norwich and Ipswich, went from Whitemoor only fifty-five miles to Pyewipe yard in Lincoln, or about 100 miles to Decoy yard in Doncaster. By the mid-1930s we were running direct trains to Edinburgh, Newcastle, Manchester, Liverpool, Leeds, Birmingham, and the whole of the freight service had been completely shaken up and reorganised to give overnight transits . . . And not only were they through trains cutting out perhaps half a day – more likely a day – in transit to those sorts of destinations, but they were also run as fitted trains. They could brake at very much higher speeds than anyone had ever done before. So the improvement in the speed of the general merchandise traffic was tremendous.'[8]

Another point was made, that productivity and wage negotiations were not linked in any organisational sense. 'Kenelm Kerr[9] and his wages negotiators were in a class of their own and it was a field in which other people did not care to tread.'[10]

Emerging from the last sentence is the point that productivity was looked at by the personnel experts almost entirely as the science or art of grading posts as low as possible, to cheapen labour costs, not as obtaining a reduction in the total work-load by a systematic review of departmental procedures. This was well brought out in one comment. 'I always felt on the LMS that the whole staff question was a little old-fashioned. Let us remember, however, that it was still a very lowly paid industry, that labour was very cheap, that the LMS had both a great strength and a problem in the fact that in the 1930s the number of staff was 225,000, which was greater than any organisation in the country except the Post Office, which is another labour-intensive industry . . . I think there was a general acceptance that the railways were a labour-intensive system anyhow. There was certainly a great deal done on the LMS in the organisation and staff department, which covered the traffic departments, to screw down both the wages and the grading of the staff.'[11]

The management's answer to falling traffics due to the combined effects of the depression and road competition was to try to reduce staff numbers and by trying, on the clerical side at any rate, to downgrade posts when they fell vacant or when there was any reorganisation. The only actual 'across the board' reductions in railway pay took place in 1928 and in 1931. In 1928 a general deduction of $2\frac{1}{2}$ per cent from all wages, salaries and directors' fees was agreed by the unions, to run initially for one year, thereafter terminable by either side on three months' notice. The cut was actually restored on 13 May 1930. But the worsening financial position of the companies induced them to propose a further cut, which took place in March 1931, the basis being $2\frac{1}{2}$ per cent off all wages, salaries and directors' fees plus a further $2\frac{1}{2}$ per cent off wages in excess of 40s per week, or salaries or fees in excess of £100 per annum. These cuts were restored by stages in 1934 and 1937.

This situation would be unthinkable in the post-war world of inflation and constantly rising wages. Does it indicate that the railway unions were not able to negotiate from strength? What had been the trend of union membership on the railway?

The Railways Act, 1921, by giving new statutory force to the machinery of negotiation, had, in Pollins's words, 'provided the legal framework for the enhanced prestige of the railway unions'.[12] But it would seem that the intensity of the industrial disputes just before and just after the 1914–18 war was not repeated after 1923 until inflation became a major factor after World War II. A managerial comment is that 'there were bitter claims and bitter disputes' but on the other hand 'I do not know that they were as bad as they became after the war [of 1939–45]'.[13]

C. Hamilton Ellis, however, attributes bitterness during the depression to the effects of the amalgamation and the consequent remoteness of authority in a much larger organisation. He refers to 'a mixture of hopelessness and sullen resentment among men who, for too long, had been serving a railway company [the LMS] to which they felt no natural loyalty, in a country which had suffered more than many from depressed trade and frustrated technical improvement'.[14]

However, the General Strike of May 1926, in which the railwaymen participated fully in support of the miners, seems to have been an isolated instance of major industrial strife on the railways. The historian of the National Union of Railwaymen, Professor Bagwell, has described how the railwaymen's response to the strike call 'was unprecedented. More railwaymen came out in sympathy with the miners on May 4th 1926 than had struck in support of their own demands on September 26, 1919.'[15] At the outset the solidarity of the wages grades staff in both the NUR and the loco men's union, the Associated Society of Locomotive Engineers & Firemen, was almost complete. The same was scarcely true of the Railway Clerks' Association, where although the RCA claimed that the response to the strike call by 6 May was satisfactory, six days later 45 per cent of the membership were reporting for duty.[16] There was, of course, considerable hostility among staff on strike to the employment by the companies of volunteer staff, but instances of violence or intimidation were few.[17] The railwaymen's strike fizzled out with an increasing drift back to work so that train services were being stepped up daily – not through the use of volunteer labour to any considerable extent – and the strike ended on 12 May. The wounds it inflicted persisted for some time because the companies made it clear that re-employment of those who had been on strike would not be unconditional and – in Bagwell's words – 'everywhere the strike was followed by part-time working and unemployment for many men'.[18]

The fear of unemployment, and also probably disillusionment with the apparent lack of union power after the collapse of the General Strike, were the most probable reasons for what otherwise would have been a surprising fall in union membership. The NUR had had 480,000 members in 1919, but by 1933 only 275,000, the reduction far exceeding the proportionate fall in the number of railway workers.

Was this damage to morale lasting? A managerial answer was negative. 'When I came in, the bitterness was still there in 1928, left over from the 1926 strike, but it was fading and by the time the early 1930s came along all the railwaymen I knew – and I agree they were mostly ex-Great Eastern men, so perhaps they were a bit easy – were loyal, dedicated, cheerful, humorous, thoroughly enjoying being railwaymen, and it didn't have an awful lot to do with it being a secure job.'[19]

A slightly different picture was painted by another commentator. 'Major industrial relations at a national level were, in my view, conducted on the railway before the war ably, logically, and with an absence of some of the spitefulness that developed afterwards.

'At local level it was different. We had some of these things that I took no pride in – the hire-and-fire business, the queues of men outside goods depots every morning waiting for work. The fact was that in the hungry 'thirties railway security was something that men dreamt about, and once they got on the railway staff they struggled desperately to remain there. It was a different world, one in which it was maybe easier to operate, but if you did not really believe in the way that things were being done it wasn't all that easy. But bear in mind that even in those days we had a form of joint consultation that was far superior to anything that was common in industry. We had our Local Departmental Committees, we had our Sectional Councils, we had communications maintained continuously between the union representatives and ourselves in a way that was an example to the rest of the world. Since the war [of 1939–45], the situation has been so entirely different, of course. Inflation made nonsense of calm industrial negotiations, and we became more and more involved in the comparison of wage rates that we never even bothered to look at in the past. We had, I think, a fairly simple test in the 'thirties. That was the comparison with the agricultural labourer, from whom so much of the railway working population was drawn . . . we worked on the principle, by and large, that if we kept a shilling a week above the agricultural workers' wage, they were all right. You would get people coming over the fence, as they called it. Life was perhaps simpler, but at the same time, from what I recall of the arguments that went on in these tribunals, the standard of advocacy was as good as, if not better than, what we had time to do afterwards.'[20]

It is of course important to consider the average earnings, and not merely the numbers employed, in assessing labour costs and productivity. Average weekly earnings of the wages staff were 67*s* 6*d* (£3·37½p) for 'conciliation'[21] grades, and 68*s* 7*d* (£3·43p) for workshop grades, in March 1924; in March 1937 the rates were 66*s* 1*d* (£3·30½p) and 70*s* 10*d* (£3·54p). But as the Ministry of Labour's cost of living index, taking March 1924 as 100, was 85 in the same month of March 1937, when average wages were calculated, real wages rose over the period, by 11·5 per cent for 'conciliation' staff and 25 per cent for workshop staff.

This scarcely bears out the gloomy picture painted by, for example, Pollins, that 'for those employed on the railways the inter-war period was one of insecurity and of falling money wages'.[22] The same author admits that 'wage rates fell by about one-quarter between 1920 and 1933 but the cost of living fell by 45 per cent'.[23] The year 1920 was a rather unsound base year to take, owing to the transient post-war boom; the period 1924 to 1937 – covering the years after grouping had been completed but before the threat of war conditions distorted the pattern – is probably a safer guide upon which general statements can be made.

It was sometimes suggested that the railways of the Underground group, later the London Passenger Transport Board, had a rather more progressive outlook on labour relations than the main line companies. They certainly paid wages that were slightly higher than the main lines; but matters were arranged so as to avoid a clash, or any serious competition between the Underground and the four companies. 'There was a document, an agreement called the "Waterloo Agreement" dating, I think, from 1919. That defined the relationship of London Transport and British Railways rates of pay and main conditions of service but the union executives wanted to keep British Railways rates and London Transport rates generally in line as well, perhaps, as the managements.'[24]

It is important to remember that this benefit was not exclusive to the Underground men; the main-line railways also recognised a cost of living requirement. 'The London allowance applied both to British Railways and to London Transport, within a certain radius of Charing Cross.'[25] It was a purely geographical arrangement. 'The Metropolitan men beyond a certain point – it may be Harrow on the Hill – did not get it. They, of course, were joint LNER/Metropolitan Line staff.'[26]

In conclusion, whatever the productivity of the traffic staff between the wars, labour productivity undoubtedly improved in workshop practice, above all on the LMS, with the introduction at Crewe and later at Derby of modern flow production lines for the construction and – more significant in terms of the relative work-load – the repair of locomotives, carriages and wagons. At Crewe works, a heavy repair of a locomotive was scheduled for completion forty-seven hours after it had been placed on the production line, whereas before the reorganisation of the works procedure a heavy repair might involve the engine being out of service for up to sixty days.[27]

The major improvement in productivity, however, was probably to be found in the use not of staff but of physical assets, particularly locomotives and wagons. These will be analysed in a later chapter.

Notes

1 On this point, see Fenelon, 'British railways since the war', *Journal of the Royal Statistical Society*, XCVI, Part III, 1933, p. 106, regarding the increase in the proportion of small consignments.

2 D. H. Aldcroft, *British Transport since 1914*, 1975, p. 40.

3 D. H. Aldcroft, *Studies in British Transport History, 1870–1970*, 1974, p. 254.

4 A. Bull (LT).
5 D. L. Munby, 'The Productivity of British Railways', *Bulletin of the Oxford University Institute of Statistics*, XXIV, No. 1, February 1962, p. 113.
6 A. J. Pearson (LMS).
7 G. R. Hayes (LNER).
8 G. F. Fiennes (LNER).
9 Kenelm Kerr, b. 1881. Entered civil service and (as Principal Private Secretary to Postmaster General) visited York on Post Office and railway business in 1912. He was recruited to the NER by Sir Eric Geddes, then Deputy General Manager, to set up the new staff conciliation scheme. Passenger Manager, NER, 1922. Assistant General Manager (Staff), LNER, 1923–46. Chairman for many years of Railways Staff Conference. Retired 1946.
10 G. R. Haynes LNER).
11 D. S. M. Barrie (LMS).
12 H. Pollins, *Britain's Railways*, 1971, p. 196.
13 A. J. Pearson (LMS).
14 C. Hamilton Ellis, *The London Midland and Scottish Railway*, 1970, p. 120.
15 P. S. Bagwell, *The Railwaymen*, 1963, p. 472.
16 *Ibid.*, p. 473.
17 The worst case was the derailment of an express at Cramlington on the LNER.
18 Bagwell, *The Railwaymen*, p. 472.
19 G. F. Fiennes (LNER).
20 A. R. Dunbar (LNER).
21 Broadly, the traffic grades and the permanent way and physical works maintenance staffs.
22 Pollins, *Britain's Railways*, p. 97.
23 *Ibid.*, p. 194.
24 A. Bull (LT).
25 *Ibid.*
26 *Ibid.*
27 See J. W. Williamson, *A British Railway behind the Scenes*, 1933, p. 37.

4

Commercial policy and charges

The criticisms of the railways in the field of commercial policy and pricing between the wars can be grouped under several heads. To begin with, there is a general allegation of lethargy and lack of enterprise, often said to have been a legacy from the past (not so very distant) when the railways had a near-monopoly of inland transport.

Next come several specific criticisms of freight charging policy. The first is that the railways failed to lower their rates so as to counter road competition effectively and retain traffic. The second is in quite the opposite direction. It is that they failed to *raise* their rates where the opportunity existed – that is, on traffics in which they still enjoyed a virtual monopoly. The third criticism is that freight charges were not cost-based, and that the railways did not trouble to ascertain the true costs of transporting different commodities under different circumstances, or try to discard unprofitable operations.

On the passenger side the criticisms are less severe, but the point is sometimes made that the railways seriously underestimated the extent of future competition from the private car. In addition, the system of reduced fares has been criticised as unselective, too complicated and too hedged around with restrictions.

Lastly, long-term commercial policy (in its broadest sense) involves the whole question of diversification into other forms of transport. Here the companies' policies of investment in both road and air transport have been criticised. This question is, however, so important that it will be covered separately, in Chapters 6 and 7.

Dealing first with the charge of lethargy, the Royal Commission on Transport in 1931 concluded that 'in the days of their monopoly, the railways had in some ways insufficiently studied the needs of the public, and their policy had become unduly conservative. The truth of the doctrine that facilities create traffic appears to have been forgotten.'[1]

Savage has suggested that 'the railways displayed a marked lack of commercial enterprise in attracting traffic in the face of competition . . . In too many cases, the convenience of the trader or passenger had been subordinated to the convenience of the company.'[2]

Two other historians, Dyos and Aldcroft, slightly qualify their comment. 'It has been suggested . . . that the railways were conservative and unenterprising and failed to take steps to meet the needs of the new situation . . . to some extent this is true particularly in the early years after the war when they were engaged with the problems of reconstruction and amalgamation. On the other hand it is perhaps a little unkind to suggest that they were "helpless spectators of their own defeat". In a number of ways the railways attempted to resuscitate their declining fortunes. They were not wholly responsible for the fact that the remedies adopted were largely without effect.'[3]

Lack of commercial enterprise was, at the end of the period, sometimes adduced to strengthen the case for nationalisation. Speaking (of course long after war conditions had intervened) in the second reading debate on the Transport Bill, 1946, Ernest Davies, MP (Labour, Enfield), said, 'the railways have failed to be enterprising . . . the railway companies today have still, more or less, a horse and buggy mentality'. Clement Davies (Liberal, Montgomery) said, 'the railway companies were not anxious to take up new ideas or put new ideas into effect'.

The LMS took up the cudgels on behalf of all the railways and in particular quoted its own record of activity. In a booklet it pointed out that as early as 1932, 'to assess the traffic potentialities, a survey was made in each of the 35 districts into which the company's territory was divided for commercial management. Valuable information was assembled of the physical features of each area, its population, its trading interests, and the various means of transport in it. In the light of this the sales arrangements were remodelled. Representatives, specially selected and trained for the purpose, were appointed, some covering an area, others a particular trade or industry, and others developing party travel through schools, churches and institutes – to supplement the day-to-day efforts of the local staff who were also given training in salesmanship.'[4]

One may feel that both the criticisms and the replies were over-stimulated by the political controversy over nationalisation, and can therefore be at least partially discounted.

But an 'insider' comment on the charge of lethargy in commercial policy included reference to the quota system for commercial performance instituted on the LMS by Ashton Davies, Chief Commercial Manager and later a Vice-President of that railway. '*Quota News* was a report on sales performance: the operating side had a corresponding journal called *On Time*.'

It was argued that these two productions were the outward sign of an aggressive commercial policy. 'I only quote these two journals as being evidence of two of the media which were in use and the personal drive of the officers concerned. The drive on the acceleration side came mostly from Ernest Lemon;[6] the drive on the commercial side came from Ashton Davies.[7] He was a most remarkable character; I was never sure how far some of the innovations we tried were in fact profitable, but certainly the drive and the enthusiasm were there. Some of the older district officers may not have liked it, I don't really know.'[8]

Another view, however, expressed some reservations about the quota system. 'The other thing which was, I think, superficial was the quota system operated by the commercial department, whereby, in a rather Russian fashion, norms and targets were set for the organisation. We even got to the stage of the production of a separate staff newspaper known as *Quota News* which gave comparisons of achievement by regions and lines and I think even down to station level on occasions. It was all rather Stakhanovite.'[9]

The LMS 'quota' system was supported by a Commercial Research Section. 'One of the biggest jobs that organisation did was to work up the container system on the LMS. From the very beginning we devised the types of container, the dimensions and so on, and the capacity. It got even more interesting when we got on to some of the specialities. For example, an outstanding case would be the development of refrigerated transport, where, in conjunction with the Technical Research Department (and in conjunction with Imperial Chemical Industries, because we used solid CO_2, dry ice) . . . we had to invent systems to get the cold, so to speak, distributed throughout the wagon and that kind of thing.'[10]

In addition, supplementing their own efforts, the main-line railways employed their subsidiary organisation, the Railway Research Service, to undertake on their behalf what would now be termed market research. 'About commercial investigations at the Railway Research Service, here are some which were done: containers; road and rail tranships; size of mineral wagons abroad; the SNCF development of suburban reversible steam working in the Paris area; claims prevention.'[11]

The introduction of containers was a field in which the Royal Commission on Transport in 1931 made quite a strong criticism. 'It is a matter of some surprise to us that containers are not more generally used; greater progress might be made in this direction.'[12] The LMS booklet pointed out that the stock of containers had been 3,200 just after the Royal Commission had made its comment but had grown to 8,000 by 1938.[13] Undoubtedly the LMS were in the lead here, owning more than half the total stock of all four companies. Initially there had been some resistance from the other railways. 'The container differential, as we called it – the history of that is rather amusing. We put that on because we found that we could get much higher rates for traffic in containers and there was a good deal of opposition from certain of the other companies in those early days, because they said that we were stealing traffic from them by supplying containers. That was one of the great features of road transport – the saving that they made, not in direct saving in transport costs but saving in the amount of packing and so on, and that is the one that the container really solved. As I say, we found that we could afford to get considerably higher rates if we needed them. We offered the other companies a kind of a dare. We said, "All right, if you don't like them we'll charge a higher rate." So in principle we invented the container differential and had a booklet of all the traffics which were normally conveyed by containers, showing the amount of the differential to be applied in any given traffic.'[14]

It was, however, admitted that the container service had problems. 'It could have been better if it had been a lot bigger, because we had wagons of twelve tons and our container payload was four. Well, that wasn't much good, and we had some of them half that size. The first types of container we developed were of two standard sizes – one virtually filled the wagon, an ordinary open wagon, and one was half the size, so that two could be loaded on an ordinary standard wagon . . . One of the first difficulties . . . was that you had got to get the wagon under a crane . . . of high capacity and . . . so many of our lesser stations — only the big ones had cranes of such high capacity; but of course that has been much improved, and what we did . . . was to get into touch with the builders of mobile cranes and get some bigger models of up to six or ten tons, which we could move by road from one station to another. They were mobile – they could travel along the road.'[15]

An LNER view was that container development had on the whole been energetically promoted. 'The railways were experimenting with primitive forms of container long before 1923, but between 1923 and 1939, to my certain knowledge, the railway companies had introduced four 'common or garden' types of containers, A, B, C and D, and they had quite a large number of special types also. They had provided freight depots with mobile cranes capable of transferring the containers from rail to road. At some of their larger stations they had gantry cranes, which were even better. It is nonsense to say that the railway companies had not developed a container system. They had thousands of them. It could be said that their standard policy of applying a container differential could have had a hampering effect, but even there, to my certain knowledge, many rates were quoted inclusive of containers, so the charge just will not stand. There ought, I think, to have been more concentration of container traffic, with container trains running between important centres and avoiding marshalling.'[16]

On the question of the container differential, the suggestion that this acted to discourage container traffic was denied. 'Railway charges, of course, were strictly on net weight. You were never charged for the weight of the container unless it was privately owned. Although it could be said in theory that there was this 10 per cent or 5 per cent differential, in practice it was so often wrapped up in an inclusive exceptional rate that the point does not really arise.'[17]

The changes in the nature of the traffic are relevant when considering criticisms of the service. Fenelon pointed out in 1933 that 'during recent years the competition of road transport and changes in the methods of internal trading in this country have forced the railways to cater more and more for traffic in small lots. Traders now demand and expect to receive special facilities for traffic passing in small consignments. Several distinct factors have combined to accentuate this tendency. Traders now work with smaller capital and shorter credit than in pre-war days; they have attempted to protect themselves from the effects of the falling price level since 1921 by carrying small stocks. Fluctuations in demand have become more frequent; fashion changes, for instance, are now spread over a much greater part of the community than in pre-war days and the demand for novelties, new designs and the like is now much more insistent than formerly. Retail traders, therefore, now carry stocks of a wider and more frequently changing variety in colour, size, pattern, shape, etc., but of each variety they carry only a small stock, relying on rapid transport facilities to replenish their stocks as need arises.

'The railways, therefore, have had to supply facilities which would meet traders' requirements, especially as this type of service can be readily given by road transport competitors. It is noticeable that where the railways have been most successful in retaining their merchandise traffic has been precisely in those services which provide fast services for small lots.[18] General parcels traffic by passenger train, as was shown earlier, has been very well maintained largely because the services provided are better than those given by road hauliers.

'Merchandise traffic by goods train has definitely tended to go in smaller lots. This has been pointed out, for example, by Sir Josiah Stamp, who has said that "the number of consignments of handled traffic per ton appears to be approximately three times what it was before the war".'[19]

Turning from general to more specific criticisms, the most commonly reiterated one is that the railways failed to retain general merchandise freight traffic in the face of road competition because they were unable or unwilling to quote competitive rates, and tended to shelter behind the legal constraints imposed on them as an excuse for not adopting a more aggressive commercial policy. Savage asserts this. 'One cannot acquit the railways of responsibility for some part of their economic misfortunes in the inter-war years. For one thing, they probably interpreted their obligations more rigidly than the law demanded.'[20]

Aldcroft agrees. 'It is often argued that the charging powers of the 1921 Act, coupled with the statutory restrictions relating to undue preference, etc., made it difficult for the railways to adopt a pricing policy which would have enabled them to have attained their net revenue. It is probable that the force of these legal impediments has been exaggerated.'[21]

Probably the fullest analysis by outside observers of the commercial handicaps under which the railways operated has been made by Milne and Laing, who point out that 'the equality and undue preference clauses lay at hand for anyone who suspected unfair discrimination, and these clauses now had a much wider range of applicability because of the amalgamation of companies. Furthermore, traders were given extensive rights of objection before the Tribunal to the making or cancellation of any such exceptional rates. Again, any trader who thought that an exceptional rate granted to another trader unduly prejudiced him, instead of going to the Railway and Canal Commission to have his rival's rate cancelled on grounds of undue preference, could apply to the Tribunal to have the same rate applied to his traffic. This concession to traders made the companies wary of granting an exceptional rate because of the fear that the particular gain from it might be outweighed by the loss of revenue involved in the extension of that exceptional rate to others.

'The obligation to publish their charges in force brought with it an unforeseen loss to the railways, for road hauliers were enabled to know both the price at which they could expect to attract traffic from the railways and the highest price they could charge their own traffics without driving consignors to seek an exceptional rate from the railways.

Moreover, the delay in making effective the exceptional rates requiring the approval of the Tribunal often allowed road hauliers, with their ability to quote snap rates, to step in and collect traffic from under the noses of the companies.'[22]

Gilbert Walker's classic study of the competition experienced by the railways between the wars described the position in rather similar terms. 'This great loss of traffic, amounting in recent years to as much again as the whole of the traffic in general merchandise, and an unspecified volume of minerals and heavy merchandise, has not been accompanied by any marked reduction in the general level of railway rates.

'If there is danger of wholesale loss of the major part of the traffic, then the policy of maintaining the rate would be short-sighted. But in many cases it must pay to keep up the rate and make no effort to retain those freights which the road hauliers have attracted away.'[23]

Walker continues with a general observation. 'Road competition has clearly not yet had any marked effect in bringing down the average level of railway rates. Nor can road competition be held solely responsible for the great increase in exceptional rates. Eighty per cent is the proportion commonly given of the traffic conveyed at exceptional rates. This is the figure for all classes of merchandise. It disguises the fact that the proportion of the higher-classed merchandise charged at exceptional rates is still less than the proportion of the lower-classed traffic, traffic, that is, which is least affected by road competition.'[24]

The railways were still clearly dominated by the idea that the lower-rated traffic could not 'bear' the standard rate because of the low value per ton of the goods carried; they did not accept that the demand for transport of (e.g.) coal was inelastic. (But see comment on this point below, p. 143.)

Having set out the legal position, and giving due weight to the difficulties facing the railway commercial officers, Milne and Laing agree with other writers that 'it is probable that the railways interpreted their obligations much more widely than the law demanded.The reasonable facilities clause did not command branch lines to be kept open at a dead loss, yet there was no vigorous policy of closure and concentration upon the development of remunerative traffics. Again, although the undue preference clause, directly and indirectly, was undoubtedly a factor limiting the ability of the railways to compete with road transport, it must not be forgotten that it was not preference as such which was prohibited but undue preference. It is not improbable that the companies exaggerated the burden of the undue preference clause on the one hand, and the willingness of the Tribunal to generalise exceptional rates and agreed charges on the other. There was a continual fear that the granting of an exceptional charge would be extended and cause a crumbling of the rate structure. The fear of the same result through the making of agreed charges may have been even greater, for it is alleged that rate-fixers paid as much attention to the difficulties they might create for rate-fixers elsewhere as to the effect on the net revenue of the company considering the charge.'[25]

Milne and Laing also considered that the outlook and training of railwaymen played a part. 'Caution in the making of exceptional rates and agreed charges, or respect for the relativity of charges, was also partly the result of the pressure of traders being allowed to impose a greater degree of uniformity on rail charges than was demanded by the undue preference clause; another part was due to the administrative problems of a large-scale undertaking, and some of the explanation lies in the growth of a generation of railwaymen who had learnt to put more emphasis on the technical problems of railway operating than on the commercial problem of competing for net revenue. It was not always appreciated that, when competition is active, commercial success is dependent as much on selling efficiency as on productive efficiency.'[26]

When discussing statutory restrictions it is sometimes overlooked that for the first five years after grouping the railway companies were, in accordance with the Railways Act, 1921, engaged in the huge task of revising the General Railway Classification of Merchandise and establishing a vast number of 'standard rates' for conveyance within each class. Their scheme had to be submitted to the Railway Rates Tribunal, which was a judicial body – a branch of the High Court – before which an elaborate procedure for hearing objections had been established by the Act, after which an 'Appointed Day' would be prescribed for bringing the new scheme into effect. That was fixed at 1 January 1928.

The railways tried to rebut the charge of inflexibility in rate-making. In its 1946 propaganda booklet the LMS pointed out that between 1923 and 1938 the company had quoted 445,000 'exceptional' rates 'either to develop business, to cater for regular flows of traffic, or to retain traffic'. In addition, over 1,000 'agreed charges' had been brought into operation since the necessary powers had been granted in the Road and Rail Traffic Act, 1933, up to the end of 1939.[27]

A rejoinder to the charge of sheltering behind statutory restrictions came from a former commercial officer. ' "Sheltering" is the wrong word. The railways were empowered towards the end to make what were called agreed charges, and that really enabled them to by-pass the restrictions provided that nobody kicked up. There were one or two objections, but no very serious ones. I would say they were not seriously hampered in the case of general merchandise traffic.'[28]

The problem of repercussions from quoting exceptional rates was, however, acknowledged to exist. 'Undoubtedly there was at one time delay in having to consult the other interested companies when perhaps a very quick reaction to road competition was necessary.'[29]

But only partial assent was given to the suggestion that rate clerks were too legalistically minded and uncommercial in their outlook. 'It is true to say that there were, among the rates people, some who were like that, but towards the end of the company period, by and large, that was no longer true.'[30]

It was also pointed out that 'the agreed charge was not the sole answer to the question of the competition with road from the rating aspect. There was a very subtle clause in that Act which said that we were not allowed to make an agreed charge for traffic in circumstances in which the situation could have been met by the grant of an exceptional rate under the provisions of the 1921 Act. That cut out all the one-load, one-consignment type of traffic which was, in my opinion, the thing on which road won all along the line.'[31]

Another view was that the statutory requirement of publication was the most severe handicap under which the railways operated. 'One haulier of my acquaintance told me quite plainly that the policy of his particular small group – and hauliers in those days were mostly fairly small groups – was to decide which route they were going to operate, ascertain the railway rates and quote rates which were 10 per cent below those rates. So publication was a handicap.'[32] Bagwell agrees that 'all that the astute road operator needed to do was to visit his nearest railway station, study the railway's charges for a comparable order, and then to underquote this railway rate just sufficiently for him to capture the business'.[33]

It is incidentally of some interest that the 'agreed charge' had been a GWR initiative. 'This was one of Sir James Milne's initiatives and was highly successful. It is very easy to overplay – the railway companies probably did this in their publicity – the extent and degree of competition. The industrial depression in its effects on carryings for heavy industry and on popular spending power was a major factor in the decline of railway profits.'[34]

Clearly there is no single or conclusive answer to the criticism that the railways failed to lower their rates effectively in the face of competition. The effects of railway activity or inactivity do, however, emerge from a study prepared by the Railway Research Service for the internal use of the railway managements. This pointed out that as regards the higher-rated traffic (i.e. classes 7–21, or the general merchandise traffic for which road transport competes), 'taking the four railways together, and comparing 1937 with 1923, receipts were down by 19 per cent, tonnage by 11 per cent, and receipts per ton-mile by 22 per cent, but ton-mileage, or the actual work done, was up by 6 per cent. The effect of road competition in this category of traffic, where it is most severe through the fact that the road haulier is not really a general carrier of all descriptions of traffic, is witnessed by the reduction in receipts per ton-mile, which gives an indication of the cost which has been incurred by the railways in their efforts to retain this higher-rated traffic.

'The problem is then one of the level of receipts rather than the volume of traffic as measured by ton-mileage; the existence of competition with other means of transport whose charges and labour conditions were, compared with the position on the railways, uncontrolled in 1937 has had a serious effect upon the financial position of the country's railway system, which, from its commencement, has undertaken the full duties of a common carrier.'[35]

The Research Service drew attention to the fall in the average receipt per ton mile. 'As regards standard freight rates, there was no change from the date they originally came into force, namely the 1st January, 1928, known as the Appointed Day under the Railways Act, 1921, until the 1st October, 1937, when an increase of approximately 5 per cent took place, as authorised by the Railway Rates Tribunal . . . Though the scales of standard charges did not change over this period of practically ten years, the average receipt per ton-mile fell considerably, partly due to the diversion of the more highly valued traffic to the roads, and partly due to the necessity for granting thousands of exceptional rates in order to retain traffic to the railways.

'The proportion of traffic carried at the standard rates has consequently fallen very considerably . . . the figures shown hereunder . . . apply to all descriptions of traffic except that in the coal class, and are compiled from data collected in a test week in March in each of the years shown:[36]

Proportion of Traffic at Standard Charges

	1930	1935
	%	%
Tonnage	24·24	17·29
Receipts	40·37	32·33'

The reference to the problem lying in 'the level of receipts' suggests a connection with the other criticism of railway commercial policy, namely a possible failure to raise rates where opportunity existed. This point has been put strongly by Aldcroft. 'On the profitable long-distance trunk routes charges could have been maintained or even raised without loss of revenue, since they were only marginally affected by road competition. On the high-cost marginal traffic routes charges should have been raised, either to cover costs or to drive traffic away so that the routes could have been closed.'[37] 'Charges should have been raised on the traffic least susceptible to substitution and on the unprofitable traffic which could have been dispensed with in the long run.'[38]

A rejoinder came from a retired commercial officer who argued that the railways 'were in more difficulty with the traffic in classes 1 to 10, which had low standard rates, some of which they would have liked to put up. It was very easy to pull rates down, but it was not at all easy to put them up.'[39]

But there was some support for the criticism from another 'inside' source. 'The old thesis used to be that we carry a lot of traffic which is basic and essential to industry at low rates, and we probably don't make any money on that. We therefore must have the higher-rated traffic which is the cream, so to speak. But in fact we know from the costing studies that a lot of the higher-rated traffic was probably a very poor payer and that most of the net revenue came from the bulk traffics in the lower reaches of the classification. Indeed, if there had been some stiffening of the rates on the traffic on which we had a virtual monopoly in the 1930s – iron ore, power station coal and those sorts of things, it could very well have made quite a lot of difference which we needed at that time.'[40]

For obvious reasons the railways in their defensive publicity made no reference to the raising of rates; but in fact an application was made – successfully – to the Railway Rates Tribunal for a general 5 per cent flat increase in 1937 – the first general increase since the new 'standard charges' came into force on 1 January 1928.

Such a general increase does not, of course, affect the criticism of failure to raise rates selectively (*a*) where this could safely have been done because the traffic was tied to rail; (*b*) where the costs of carrying the traffic would have justified an increase. The suggestion that selective increases should have been made was supported by the admission that 'it could very well have made quite a lot of difference which we needed at that time'.[41]

But in so far as the lower-rated traffics were candidates for such treatment it is relevant to refer to the Railway Research Service analysis which dealt with the trends in the 'Coal, Coke and Patent Fuel' class of traffic, the one most completely captive to rail and hence the one in which the possibility of increasing charges would seem, at any rate in theory, to be strongest. The service commented that 'coal and coke traffic is, to a considerable extent, affected by the export and bunkering trade, especially in the case of the Great Western and the London and North Eastern Railways. Of recent years, this trade has been seriously affected by political considerations, and again such events are outside the power of railway companies to control.

'The Great Western has suffered more seriously than the other railways so far as coal and coke traffic is concerned when 1937 results are compared with those of 1923, and, with the exception of the Southern Railway, whose figures were aided by the development of the Kent coalfield, the results for 1929 were considerably below those of 1923. This leeway has not been made up during the last nine years, although 1937 results were a great improvement on the figures for 1933, when the lowest point was touched.

'Even ton-mileage, which has risen considerably in the case of merchandise traffic, has shown no resilience so far as coal and coke traffic is concerned, in part due to the strong coastal competition, especially between north-east coast ports and the London area, bulk cargoes being carried by water to points on the Thames above London, in fact London coal is becoming increasingly seaborne . . . Expressed briefly compared with 1923, export and bunker tonnage has decreased by 48 million tons, a loss offset to the extent of 14 million tons by increased home consumption.'[42]

The implication is that higher rates on export and bunker coal might have rendered these commodities uncompetitive and reduced traffics. Equally, industrial and house-coal traffic was to a considerable extent subject to competition from coastwise shipping, which restricted the ability to raise rates.

An element which certainly also needs to be taken into account is the presence on the railway Boards of certain directors who had interests in coal, iron and steel and who would have objected to discrimination (as it would have seemed) against their industries. One anecdote from the Great Western illustrates the problem of these relationships. 'A year or so before Pole decided to go, the export of coal from South Wales was falling off, overseas markets were being lost and the coal owners were coming to Paddington for reduced rates from the collieries to the South Wales docks, pressing for reduced rates, which was very difficult to concede. Pole had the idea that we would voluntarily concede slightly higher prices for locomotive coal provided the coal owners would utilise that money to reduce the price at which they were offering export coal. Rightly or wrongly, they were saying that they were losing export orders on the turn of a penny, and Pole had this idea that he couldn't reduce the rates because there were repercussions in other directions but if we voluntarily gave them a little more for our locomotive coal, if that fund was used to lower the export price, that might stimulate the traffic. Now that idea was hailed as tip-top by those directors on our Board who were coal owners. And we had a number of them that we inherited from the South Wales railways on amalgamation. Those who were not coal owners didn't think so much of the idea, and as a result the Board became divided and there was a good deal of hostility between one side and the other at that time.'[43]

The last point on freight traffic is a general criticism of the absence of any scientific costing system. Aldcroft suggests that 'the problem was aggravated by the increasing degree of cross-subsidisation which inevitably followed from amalgamation, and this no doubt reduced the incentive to determine the costs of specific services . . . Charges were rarely adjusted to take account of variation in costs of operation.'[44] To this one trenchant reply was: 'I am quite sure that the railways have lost a very large quantity of traffic through fussing about costs and trying to calculate direct costs. With a railway I am quite sure that it pays, on the whole, to maximise the use of the tracks and the rolling stock in terms of locomotion and vehicles, and you cannot improve upon the Acworth dictum of charging what the traffic will bear and getting as much traffic as you can within sensible limits – full stop.'[45]

Another reply was to the effect that in fact there *was* a considerable knowledge of relative operating costs. 'It should not be thought that the railway companies were without knowledge of the relative costs of minerals and the more highly rated merchandise traffics, nor, I believe, did the classification of traffic entirely ignore cost. In the famous phrase of Gilbert Walker, "the cream is at the bottom of the bottle". The railway companies were aware that although the mineral traffics, classes 1–6, were relatively lowly rated, they did well in terms of net revenue out of those traffics.'[46]

Aldcroft argues that variation in the costs of individual routes, as well as of individual types of traffic, should have been taken into account. 'The railways made little proper attempt to adapt their pricing policy to meet the changed conditions of the period . . . partly through ignorance about operating costs of individual routes and services of the system and partly because of the restrictions imposed on their powers of charging by the 1921 Act, though . . . this excuse for inaction has worn a little thin with time.'[47]

This criticism is also expressed in another way by Dyos and Aldcroft. 'The important point is whether the actual reductions in charges were made in a way to secure the best results. Quite clearly this was not the case. Many of the changes were made indiscriminately and failed to differentiate sufficiently between good and bad traffic. Had greater attention been paid when making the concessions to the variations in the elasticity of demand for the transport services in question and the costs of operation, the outcome in the long run might have been more satisfactory. As it was, many of the reductions were less than useless in helping the railways to pay their way. In some cases charges were too high and in others too low.'[48]

This criticism can take another form – that the railways' lack of a traffic costing system led them to neglect the possibility of closing unremunerative lines. Savage makes the point clearly. 'The principle of grouping under the 1921 Act and the obligation to afford reasonable facilities did not compel them to keep open branch lines that operated at a certain loss. Yet the companies did not follow any general policy of closing little-used and badly paying lines.'[49]

Aldcroft agrees. 'The scope for further economies by rationalising services and pruning the uneconomic parts of the system was enormous, but neither course of action was seriously contemplated by the railways in this period. Perhaps the main fault of the railways was that they still placed great emphasis on retaining as much traffic as possible regardless of whether or not it was profitable.'[50] He points out that the amalgamations had increased cross-subsidisation, which is true only in territorial terms – e.g. the former Great Central Railway's traffics were to some extent supported by those on the former Great Northern – but this is unlikely to have had any effect upon charging policy: and it is hard to see how – in Aldcroft's words – 'this no doubt reduced the incentive to determine the costs of specific services'. One would have expected a large, 'rationalised' undertaking to be *more* cost-conscious because more scientific in its approach. This argument is supported by an 'inside' comment. 'The question of costing very much concerned the railway companies. Just before the war a financial and commercial committee, on which Dashwood served, undertook a very detailed cost study and a survey of the attribution of the costs to different streams of traffics and operations . . . The companies were not unaware of the problems. It is very easy . . . to overestimate the degree to which it is possible to identify separately the costs of particular lines or particular traffics. There is always this large element of joint or common cost which has to be taken into account. But I do not think that if the criterion taken is gross revenue plus passengers or freight carried, on particular lines, there was any substantial reason to suppose that a policy of closure of lines would, at that time, have paid dividends. After the war the change in industrial pattern, the much greater development of road freight transport and the huge increase in car ownership forced the issue of withdrawal from certain parts of the total railway system.'[51]

On the passenger side historians have on the whole been less critical. However, Aldcroft is sharply critical of fares policy. 'Cheap fares were granted on all routes irrespective of the degree of competition and eventually nearly all passengers were travelling at reduced rates . . . on some of the short-distance and cross-country routes . . . there was a strong case for pricing the traffic out of the market.'[52]

The Research Service study bears upon this point to some extent. 'One may stress the continuous fall in the proportion of receipts at full fares, namely from 56 per cent in 1923 to 35·3 per cent in 1929 and 11·9 per cent in 1937. Concerning the number of journeys, this comparative fall of the percentage at full fares has been 31·5, 13·0 and 6·5 respectively. On the other hand, there has been a practically continuous growth, both relatively and absolutely, in traffic, whether measured by numbers or by receipts, classed as "excursion, week-end, etc.". This designation includes monthly return tickets which have, in effect, replaced ordinary return tickets, since they have in recent years been issued, subject to a small minimum distance in most areas, between any pair of stations, and have no restrictions as to the trains by which they are available.'[53] In fact it is almost impossible to determine whether the reductions – by no means standard between the companies – were sufficiently selective. There was, however, a continuous process of testing demand by experiment.

Before the war the Royal Commission's Final Report was critical of the facilities rather than the economics of passenger policy. 'Special fares for excursions, etc., are too often hedged about with special conditions. The public objects to irritating conditions. A general revision and lowering of fares by the railway companies would do far more towards the recovery of their passenger traffic than the methods adopted by them at present.'[54]

During the second reading debate on the 1946 Transport Bill the Chancellor of the Exchequer claimed that the poor quality of passenger travel by rail in Britain was 'one reason why the tourist traffic is not so easily attracted here'. Special criticisms were directed at the railways on a constituency basis. For example, the member for Enfield attacked the condition of Liverpool Street station; the members for Bradford and Hull respectively complained of poor service for those cities. But there was little informed comment upon passenger charging policy.

An 'inside' view on the general attitude of the railways to future demand was: 'I do not think either the main-line railway companies or London Transport fully appreciated the inroads which private car traffic was going to make into their passenger traffic. I believe, with hindsight, that they could have anticipated to a greater extent than they did what the influence of private car traffic would be, because America was roughly ten years ahead in the ownership of private cars per hundred or per million households, and already in America railway commuter traffic, railway suburban traffic, railway inter-city passenger traffic was suffering quite heavily from private car competition.'[55]

A different view could, however, be taken. 'On car ownership, I did, during these years, hear the view expressed that the spread of road transport, and in particular the private car, led to greater mobility and dispersal of the population. This in turn was a stimulus to overall transport demand from which the railway services benefited in some degree, particularly the parcels service.'[56]

As for the criticisms about lack of enterprise on the passenger side, the LMS, although primarily a freight line, replied vigorously in its propaganda booklet. 'A variety of cheap bookings and other travel inducements were offered to the public, a notable development being the institution of monthly return tickets giving third-class travel at a penny a mile by any train on any day within a month which carried the same conditions as ordinary tickets. Other facilities included a wide range of day, half-day, evening and "guaranteed" excursions; holiday contract or "10/- [50p] run-about" tickets; holiday camping coaches; inclusive bookings of several kinds for the pleasure-seeker; bulk travel vouchers for business firms; weekly season tickets for regular short-distance journeys; educational excursions for school-children and their teachers; reduced rates for private motor cars accompanying passengers; and the purchase of rail tickets by instalments under a "save-to-travel" scheme.

'The development of an extensive cheap fare policy naturally had its reaction upon the ordinary bookings and it necessitated considerable judgment to hold the balance so that the optimum net revenue might be secured to the company. The position was rendered difficult by external factors, such as the reduction in the incomes of the travelling public during and following periods of trade depression and labour unrest, the rapid growth in the use of privately owned motor cars, and the intense competition from other forms of transport not subject to the restrictions imposed by Parliament on the railway companies.'[57]

The Southern Railway enjoyed relative immunity from the criticism levied against the other railways, since it had started from a low point in public esteem and by energetic management, concentrating upon improved services largely through electrification, was by the outbreak of war probably the most highly regarded of the four groups. In the early years it had been the target of an adverse press campaign which, C.

Hamilton Ellis reports,[58] started in 1924 with the abandonment of the fast Portsmouth service on the LBSC side and concentration on the LSW route. This was followed by a campaign of criticism of the suburban services, the condition and age of passenger coaches and locomotives, and unpunctuality, being the main targets.

This early unpopularity was something that the Southern had to live down: and that it certainly did, if one can judge from the omission of any severe criticism from economists, historians or even politicians in the heat of debate.

If one seeks to set in perspective both the criticisms of railway commercial policies and the defences that have been put forward, it is probably helpful to distinguish between contemporary and subsequent arguments. Between the wars criticism does not seem to have dealt with the same issues as those discussed by modern historians writing with the benefit of hindsight. Even the Royal Commission on Transport ignored the questions of selective increases in charges, the need for traffic costing, and the hampering effect of statutory control of charges. The existing framework of classification, 'standard' and 'exceptional' rates, was taken for granted.

Recent historians have implied that the railways should have broken out of their straitjacket much sooner. It was of course only in 1938 that they presented the government with their demand for a 'Square Deal', or complete freedom from obsolete restrictions on their charging powers. But the opposition from industry to any such liberation was strong. 'They had umpteen committees of inquiry. They brought in all sorts of politicians to master it – people like Salter and those sort of people, and all that that did was to delay freedom, because to these committees of inquiry all sort of opposition came from people like Traffic Managers who were fearing that if this relaxation were granted then they would be charged more. There was a considerable army of those sort of people bringing pressure to bear: Unilever were doing it; Lever Brothers were doing it; even road competitors were doing it! I can go through the various firms who had experts opposing any relaxation at all. And so the railways struggled with this, fought for freedom, got authority to make agreed charges which gave them limited freedom. Up to the nationalisation period in the late 1940s they were still struggling with the shackles of the old restrictions. They were only taken off after nationalisation. It is incredible that it should have been so, but nobody in the railway service – and it had some of the most brilliant expositors – nobody ever succeeded in persuading government that the restrictions were out of time and should be removed.'[59]

This comment may help to illustrate the background to some decision-making by railway managements which, at long range, and with hindsight, may seem to have been insufficiently farsighted.

Notes

1 Royal Commission on Transport, *Final Report* (Cmd. 3751, 1931), Summary of Conclusions, para. 536.
2 T. C. Barker and C. I. Savage, *An Economic History of Transport in Britain*, 1975, p. 158.
3 H. J. Dyos and D. H. Aldcroft, *British Transport*, 1969, p. 329.
4 LMS, *A Record of Large-scale Organisation and Management, 1923–46*, 1946, p. 16.
5 D. S. M. Barrie (LMS).
6 Sir Ernest J. H. Lemon, OBE, 1884–1954. Carriage and Wagon Superintendent, LMS, 1927. Chief Mechanical Engineer, 1931. Vice-President (Commercial and Operating), 1932–43. Director General of Aircraft Production, Air Ministry, 1938–40.
7 Ashton Davies, CVO, OBE, 1874–1958. Superintendent of the Line, LYR, 1919–21. General Superintendent, Western Division, LMS, 1923. Chief Commercial Manager, 1932–38. Vice-President, 1938–44.
8 D. S. M. Barrie (LMS).
9 P. E. Garbutt (LMS).
10 J. R. Pike (LMS).
11 C. E. Whitworth (Railway Research Service).
12 Royal Commission on Transport, 1931, para. 536.
13 *Ibid.*, p. 17.
14 J. R. Pike (LMS).
15 *Ibid.*
16 A. A. Harrison (LNER).

17 *Ibid.*
18 Later costing studies (e.g. those published in the British Transport Commission's Annual Report for 1951, pp. 71–5) have shown how unlikely it was that this traffic was profitable!
19 K. G. Fenelon, 'British Railways since the War', *Journal of the Royal Statistical Society*, XCVI, Part III, 1933, p. 22.
20 Barker and Savage, *An Economic History of Transport*, p. 158.
21 D. H. Aldcroft, *British Railways in Transition*, 1968, p. 59.
22 A. M. Milne and A. Laing, *The Obligation to Carry*, 1956, p. 30.
23 G. Walker, *Road and Rail*, 1942, p. 124.
24 *Ibid.*, p. 126.
25 *The Obligation to Carry*, p. 33.
26 *Ibid.*, p. 34.
27 *A Record of Large-scale Organisation*, p. 18.
28 A. A. Harrison (LNER).
29 *Ibid.*
30 *Ibid.*
31 J. R. Pike (LMS).
32 A. W. Tait (GWR).
33 P. S. Bagwell, *The Transport Revolution from 1770*, 1974, p. 254.
34 A. W. Tait (GWR).
35 Railway Research Service, *The Main Line Railways of Great Britain, 1923–37*, 1938, Summary History and Statistics, p. 33.
36 *Ibid.*, p. 6.
37 D. H. Aldcroft, *Studies in British Transport History, 1870–1970*, 1974, p. 234.
38 D. H. Aldcroft, *British Transport since 1914*, 1975, p. 40.
39 A. A. Harrison (LNER).
40 G. F. Fiennes (LNER).
41 A. R. Dunbar (LNER).
42 Railway Research Service, *The Main Line Railways*, p. 34.
43 H. H. Phillips (GWR).
44 Aldcroft, *British Transport since 1914*, p. 40.
45 A. A. Harrison (LNER).
46 A. W. Tait (GWR).
47 Aldcroft, *British Transport since 1914*, p. 40.
48 Dyos and Aldcroft, *British Transport*, p. 337.
49 Barker and Savage, *An Economic History of Transport*, p. 158.
50 Aldcroft, *British Transport since 1914*, p. 40.
51 A. W. Tait (GWR).

52 Aldcroft, *British Railways in Transition*, p. 59.
53 Railway Research Service, *The Main Line Railways*, p. 32.
54 Royal Commission on Transport, *Final Report*, Summary of Conclusions, para. 536.
55 A. Bull (LT).
56 A. W. Tait (GWR).
57 *A Record of Large-scale Organisation*, p. 17.
58 C. Hamilton Ellis, *British Railway History*, vol. II, 1959, p. 320.
59 A. J. Pearson (LMS).

5

The physical assets

Allegations which are difficult to support by factual data, and equally difficult to refute, relate to the physical condition of the railways before nationalisation. The most vehement were voiced by Labour politicians. In the second reading debate on the Transport Bill, 1946, for instance, the Chancellor of the Exchequer, Dr Hugh Dalton, prefaced his well known and often quoted reference to 'a very poor bag of assets' by several specific criticisms. 'The railways,' he said 'are in very poor physical shape. The permanent way is badly worn. The rolling stock is in a state of great dilapidation. The railway stations and their equipment are a disgrace to the country.' In the same debate the Minister of Transport, Alfred Barnes, said, 'Many of our railway stations, and main line termini, occupy the most important sites in London, and great provincial cities. Very often they are depressing places to arrive at . . .' This theme was enlarged upon by J. Irving (Labour, North Tottenham) and other Labour members.

Two points are relevant when considering these and similar criticisms. The first is that they were largely voiced to justify a political decision that had already been taken, namely to nationalise the railways; the second, that to some extent they were directed at conditions that were a result of the war rather than of the companies' pre-war policies.

However, in the same debate the Lord President of the Council, Herbert Morrison, did claim specifically that 'a good deal of the British railway system was really not very creditable before the war. There was great difficulty with the rolling stock, and there was much sheer obsolescence.' The Minister of Transport echoed this attack on behalf of the government.

Such criticisms were not confined to politicians; even a well informed railway historian, C. Hamilton Ellis, has written about the LMS in the 1920s in these terms. 'The stations, best on the Caledonian and the Midland lines, were ancient, and getting shabby, and the same applied to much of the rolling stock . . .'[1] 'In the middle 1930s, apart from its crack services, the LMS had become a shabby and even a dirty railway . . . maintenance was down to the safe limit; breakdowns were not infrequent, and punctuallity, especially of the West Coast expresses, was bad.'[2]

Whatever the state of the LMS, it was energetically denied that the GWR had major shortcomings. 'It was the policy of the Great Western to set aside substantial renewal funds for track and rolling stock, and I would have thought the record in both cases showed that sufficient funds were set aside. The company's policy, certainly, in maintaining and renewing existing track and in carrying through a forward-looking policy of standardisation of locomotives – thus reducing costs, backed, incidentally, by some very good costing records – enabled the company to meet what was required for rolling stock and a certain amount of new investment in such things as diesel railcars or additional locomotives without serious difficulty.'[3]

The criticisms of the politicians and even that of Hamilton Ellis were no doubt largely subjective judgements even where formed by observation, and may have been coloured to some extent by political views or prejudice. But they are broadly endorsed by Bagwell, who comments that 'a consequence of the railways' meagre financial returns was their failure to invest adequately in modernisation. Although gross investment amounted to £283 million between 1920 and 1938, this was an insufficient sum even to cover proper depreciation and replacement, especially in respect of the permanent way. The net result was thus a disinvestment of £125 million over the 19 years . . . The general inadequacy of inter-war investment masked some important exceptions. The Southern Railway invested nearly £14 million in the electrification of its rail network in the 1930s . . .'[4]

Bagwell's calculation of gross investment presumably includes capital expenditure plus renewals of assets. The statutory form of the railway accounts over the period provides a capital receipts and expenditure account, only the balance of which goes into the balance sheet. Capital receipts had been £55 million between 1923 and 1933: but the financing of new works on a large scale after 1935 was put in hand on the basis of funds raised not by the railways but by the London Electric Transport Finance Corporation Ltd and the Railway Finance Corporation Ltd, organisations which had been 'specially set up for the purpose of raising new capital to carry out the two large programmes of improvement, electrification, rolling stock, widenings and the like, approved under the London Passenger (Agreement) Act of 1935 and the Railways (Agreement) Act of the same year. By these means, the railways were enabled to benefit through the raising of capital at the low "gilt-edged" rate of less than 3 per cent, there being a guarantee of capital and interest by the Government, while the Government itself benefited through the starting of important schemes of work at a time when they would not otherwise have been undertaken, thus relieving, to some extent, unemployment in many industries and various areas. The railways themselves could only have raised such large sums at interest rates which would not have allowed works to have proved remunerative.

'Under the Development (Loan Guarantees and Grants) Act of 1929, the railways undertook a considerable number of major capital improvement schemes; in this case, Government grants being available, up to maximum period of fifteen years, representing interest on the capital outlay incurred on the approved works. This represents the nearest approach to financial assistance which has ever occurred since the formation of the four main line companies.'[5]

An attempt to assess and quantify 'disinvestment' in the physical assets has been made by Aldcroft.[6] He argues that whilst gross investment (including renewals) was quite high over the inter-war years, the annual rate of depreciation (based on arbitrary life cycles assigned to different classes of asset) exceeded gross investment every year, so that there was a continuous process of disinvestment. The table upon which he chiefly relies is drawn from Feinstein and is reproduced here (table 3[7]).

Table 3
Investment in British railways, 1920–38
(at constant 1930 prices)

	Gross fixed capital formation in all assets (£m.)	*Depreciation* (£m.)	*Net capital formation* (£m.)		
			Total	*Permanent way and works*	*Rolling stock*
1920	11·0	21·5	−10·5	−9·7	−0·1
1921	13·4	21·4	−8·0	−7·9	0·1
1922	10·3	21·3	−11·0	−7·1	−3·8
1923	12·1	21·1	−9·0	−5·1	−2·6
1924	15·2	21·2	−6·0	−5·9	0·6
1925	17·3	21·3	−4·0	−6·1	2·4
1926	15·4	21·4	−6·0	−7·6	1·5
1927	18·6	21·6	−3·0	−4·9	2·3
1928	15·6	21·6	−6·0	−7·1	1·5
1929	12·6	21·6	−9·0	−9·3	1·3
1930	15·6	21·6	−6·0	−6·2	0·1
1931	16·5	21·5	−5·0	−2·6	−2·0
1932	15·4	21·4	−6·0	−3·1	−2·9
1933	8·9	21·5	−12·6	−8·8	−3·3
1934	11·4	21·4	−10·0	−8·4	−0·6
1935	14·4	21·4	−7·0	−7·9	1·4
1936	17·6	21·6	−4·0	−6·3	2·7
1937	19·7	21·7	−2·0	−5·2	3·9
1938	21·7	21·7	0·0	−2·8	2·5

Note: Depreciation based on an assumed life of assets as follows: permanent way, 100 years; buildings and works, 60 years; rolling stock, 33 years and power and plant, 25 years. Rolling stock estimates do not take account of privately owned wagons.

Source: C. H. Feinstein, *Domestic Capital Formation in the United Kingdom, 1920–1938* (1965) table 9.10, pp. 150–1.

Aldcroft argues that net investment in each year was negative, and the total disinvestment for the period as a whole amounted to £125 million,[8] although he admits that such estimates can only be very approximate since they are based on a hypothetical life-cycle of railway assets.[9]

It is perhaps a pity that, in using Feinstein's figures, he does not quote *in extenso* from the former's lengthy explanations regarding the extreme reserve with which the figures must be used. Feinstein begins by explaining that his estimates for the permanent way and works 'raise in a very clear form the problems which arise where assets (*a*) do not have a normal life-cycle but are subject to a long series of expenditures which have simultaneously some of the characteristics of maintenance, of partial renewal and of modernisation and improvement; and (*b*) are owned by enterprises which adopted the renewals system of accounting.'[10] He agrees that 'we have inevitably to adopt a number of fairly arbitrary methods'.[11] Later Feinstein refers to 'assets where the awkward cases are the rule rather than the exception'.[12]

His caution is, to say the least, justified. For the enquiry whether, over a period of years, there has been a net gain in investment, or alternatively a net loss (i.e. 'disinvestment'), information is essential under several heads. First, one needs a figure for the 'value' of the fixed assets at the beginning of the period, which can be based either on estimated earning power, on original cost less depreciation, or on value in alternative uses ('opportunity cost'). Next, one needs to know how this original value is eroded, whether by age, by weather, by wear and tear, or merely by changing techniques leading to obsolescence and loss of profitability.

Against this process of diminishing values one has to set expenditure on preservation of capital assets through renewals and the net additions to the stock of capital goods, over and above those displaced as not required.

The statutory form of railway accounts in the period under review certainly gives full information about expenditure upon both repairs and renewals, and sets out the capital expenditure on fixed assets, less items written out of capital account. But it does *not* give the essential information about original values and the annual loss of value requiring replacement, as would be the case where a company applies a correct rate of depreciation to a set of correctly valued fixed assets. The 'renewals' principle of accounting, as Feinstein recognises[13] in his explanatory notes, makes it difficult to employ such a simple formula. Under the Double Account system required by Parliament at that date, there was provision for renewals on a replacement-cost basis through renewal funds built up from annual revenue, but capital expenditure and capital receipts were recorded separately, only the balance by which capital expenditure exceeded capital receipts or vice versa being carried to the balance sheet.

If then one seeks to establish the 'value' of railway fixed assets at any time, the chief figure available is the historic cost shown in the capital expenditure account. But this has little or no relevance to later value. It does not discount earning capacity, nor does it reflect in any way 'opportunity cost', since most railway assets have no alternative uses. Nor is it first cost less depreciation.

The bulk of the railway network exists as a result of investment undertaken between 1830 and 1870, at price levels, and using constructional techniques, very different from those of the 1920s or 1930s. It is therefore questionable whether any real significance can be placed upon Feinstein's estimate[14] that at 1938 prices the 'first-cost value' of the permanent way and works was £1,536 million, compared with the capital expenditure upon these items shown in the *Railway Returns* of the Ministry of Transport for 1938 as £854 million.

But even if such a notional 'first-cost value' is accepted as a working hypothesis, how can one measure the annual loss of value from the effects of (*a*) lapse of time, (*b*) exposure to weather, (*c*) use, (*d*) obsolescence? To assign arbitrary lives to different groups of assets and then to calculate a 'straight line' depreciation provision is unrealistic. Feinstein assigns a life of 100 years to 'permanent way' and sixty years to structures, against which he calculates a notional annual depreciation requirement. But in fact the life of the 'formation' – embankments, cuttings, tunnels, etc. – is quite indefinite. These assets have really been incorporated into the landscape. Even tunnels, although requiring partial or occasionally complete relining at some time or other, are otherwise almost immortal.

(The only major British example of a tunnel being replaced after a century or so of use is that of the Woodhead tunnel through the Pennines, where a new double-track tunnel replaced the old twin single-bore tunnels in 1953.) And bridges, viaducts, and many buildings have mostly far longer lives than sixty years, though stations may well require a certain amount of modernisation, ranging from mere 'face-lifting' to reconstruction, to meet changing traffic conditions. As for the track, widely different lives can be assigned to rails and fastenings, sleepers and ballast – depending on a whole range of factors, including atmospheric conditions, the nature of the subsoil and the density of traffic. No single annual rate of depreciation on first cost has any general validity.

One can therefore only seek to consider whether the actual expenditure upon repairs and renewals was adequate properly to maintain the assets that continued to be required in productive use, and whether the capital expenditure upon new assets exceeded the amounts written out of capital in respect of assets no longer required.

At this point it is useful to quote a trenchant comment from a senior railway officer.[15] 'I find the Feinstein table quite irrelevant to the facts of life although interesting to theorise about. . . . in the years 1920 to 1938 . . . failure to disinvest would have reflected a failure in management to realise the economies possible as a result of the amalgamation and the drive to achieve operational efficiency with maximum utilisation of assets and the consequential run down of those surplus to requirements.

'The elimination of wasteful competition following the pooling and inter-company closer working schemes were also factors which gave scope for reduction in the assets we were obliged to maintain.'

There is, of course, a further point here. The railways certainly closed some unremunerative branch lines between the wars – e.g. the Southern's hopelessly uneconomic 'light railway' branch from Basingstoke to Alton.[16] But they were not relieved by the Railways Act 1921, of the obligation to afford 'reasonable facilities' for freight traffic, first imposed in 1854; and this may well have had a 'blanket' effect in discouraging them from discarding sections of line (with consequent 'disinvestment') to the full extent that a ruthlessly commercial approach might have dictated.

After the grouping the companies expected at first to earn the 'standard revenues' assigned to them under the Railways Act, 1921. In this, of course, they were disappointed. One therefore needs to consider whether shortfalls in revenue led to a serious reduction in maintenance provisions.

The rate of annual expenditure upon 'maintenance of way and works' (which presumably is what Feinstein means by 'permanent way') certainly fell, up to the beginning of the economic depression, by about 9 per cent. There was also a reduction of 6 per cent in the case of rolling stock. After 1929 the reductions were more marked, presumably reflecting the fall in traffic during the depression, as well as the economies referred to above, derived from amalgamation and more effective workshop practices.

Table 4
The four grouped companies' maintenance expenditure (£ million)

Year	*Way and works*	*Rolling stock*
1923	23·5	27·6
1924	23·0	27·4
1925	22·6	27·2
1926	19·4	23·4
1927	21·2	27·2
1928	21·1	25·4
1929	21·0	26·0
1930	19·7	24·9
1931	18·1	22·4

Source: Ministry of Transport *Railway Returns.*

The figures in table 4 do not suggest any major changes in policy or draconian economy measures but rather a modest realisation of the 'economies of scale' following amalgamation – and (particularly on the LMS) the benefits of improved workshop practice in rolling stock maintenance.

The figures include three elements: repairs, partial renewals and full renewals. The borderline between these categories is not always clear. A locomotive undergoing a 'heavy repair' was in fact being virtually restored to new condition. A 'renewal' might mean that a virtually new locomotive had been placed in the stock, possibly no more than the wheels and coupling rods of the original being incorporated in the 'renewed' engine.

In way and structures, 'repairs' might include simple preservation expenditure such as painting or renewal of portions of a building without extension: 'renewals' might involve extension or remodelling of a building.

Turning to consider capital expenditure, after allowing for items displaced and written out, capital expenditure rose between 1923 and 1931, the period of Feinstein's calculations, by a net total of £32·7 million on the railway proper, excluding ancillary businesses. These figures are of course net after allowing for amounts written out of capital representing the historic cost of assets displaced without replacement.

The capital expenditure in most cases represents only the 'betterment' element in the total outlay, in which the replacement cost of the original asset is deducted from the outlay and charged to a renewal fund, only the excess cost of the new asset being charged to capital as 'betterment'.

Neither of these accountancy practices yields a calculation of 'investment' or 'capital formation' in the sense used by economists, namely outlay upon a durable asset – whether an addition to the existing stock or a replacement of a life-expired asset.

Aldcroft comments that 'by and large it was the permanent way which was neglected'.[17] But this statement is open to challenge on a number of grounds. First of all, the chief engineering officers of the railways were required to sign a certificate every year, for the companies' Boards of Directors and auditors, to the effect that the physical assets had been maintained in a proper manner.[18] Secondly, the companies were required to furnish evidence every year to the Railway Rates Tribunal regarding the 'efficiency and economy' with which their undertakings had been managed during the previous year. Lastly, the annual reports of the Chief Inspecting Officers of Railways in the Ministry of Transport offered an opportunity to comment upon any shortcomings in maintenance standards affecting safety.

All these formal reports produced annual confirmation that the essential elements of maintenance – permanent way, structures, traction and rolling stock – had *not* been neglected. But at the same time the company managements had been under pressure to effect economies, particularly on the LMS and the LNER. This was bound to have an impact upon maintenance standards in some ways, such as the station painting programmes and hand cleaning of passenger carriages.

The impact probably varied. 'I should suspect that there would be quite a difference between the different companies. I think the Great Western probably kept up pretty well because they were in a better financial position. The LMS – I think fairly well. The LNER . . . had to try and skimp and save money where they could.'[19] But this former LNER officer did not agree with Aldcroft's remark that 'by and large it was the permanent way which was neglected'. 'On the LNER it was not true of track maintenance.'[20]

One may wonder whether 'investment' can be assessed in a qualitative sense, if the infrastructure was improved through new techniques of construction. So far as buildings and other structures are concerned, the inter-war years do not appear to have thrown up any very important developments in the techniques of the building and construction industries affecting the railways. Signalling, however, was moving into a new phase in which power signalboxes were replacing manual ones, especially at large terminal stations such as Waterloo, Charing Cross, Cannon Street and Paddington, with the Southern Railway in the van because of the advantages of colour-light multiple-aspect signals for intensive suburban electric train service operation.

The permanent way did not change very greatly, though the 45 ft rail was supplanted almost everywhere by the 60 ft rail, and a number of improvements were introduced, on an experimental basis. Trial lengths of flat-bottom rail were laid, replacing the traditional bullhead type resting in cast iron chairs. Some 120 ft lengths of rail were put into experimental use in 1937. The LMS pamphlet listed 'the welding of switches and crossings *in situ*, thereby materially prolonging their lives; new creosoting methods; the mechanisation of material depots; the use of steel keys, in place of timber, which minimise rail creep; mechanised plant for unloading wagons; the reconditioning of worn fishplates to improve the joints of partly worn rails; the adoption of standard designs of rail, ballast and sleeper wagons; new designs of locomotive water troughs which are easier to install and maintain and cause less wastage of water; the use of mobile maintenance gangs with motor trollies; the standardisation of fencing; and the adoption of "two level" junctions to enable the superelevation to be carried right through the junction, with increased comfort in travel and relaxation of speed restrictions. At one main line junction the permissible speed of trains has by this means been increased from 30 to 55 m.p.h. with more comfortable riding.'[21]

Minor and experimental improvements included the use of two-hole fishplates in place of the standard four-hole pattern, discontinued after an extensive trial on several railways; and the 'Ellson joint', named after the Chief Engineer of the Southern Railway, and used on parts of that system. It was designed to reduce batter by wheels at rail joints by machining the ends of the rails so that they fitted together in an S shape; but it proved difficult to manufacture and hence too expensive.

In all, the LMS pamphlet claimed, 'the track of 1923 could not have stood the stress of later years . . . by trains travelling at 60 m.p.h. or over, start to stop'.[22]

These technological changes may or may not constitute 'investment' in financial terms, but realistically, they add up to an infrastructure improved in many important components.

So far as movable assets – traction and rolling stock – are concerned, Feinstein's calculations (which Aldcroft accepts and quotes) are based upon 'investment' or 'disinvestment' resulting from capital and renewals expenditure together which respectively exceeds or falls short of a notional depreciation requirement. This latter is based upon assigning an arbitrary life of thirty-three years to locomotives and rolling stock, which is not so far removed from the railways' own former basis for the purpose of calculating renewals provision requirements. On this basis Feinstein's table shows that in most years between 1920 and 1938 there was net investment in traction and rolling stock.

There is no reason to doubt that, by and large, the railway companies did possess a more 'valuable' asset in their traction and rolling stock at the outbreak of war in 1939 than in 1923. In this the major electrification schemes of the Southern Railway were an important element. The Great Western had carried out consistent locomotive, carriage and wagon building programmes which adequately refreshed the stock position. The LMS had embarked upon a major overhaul of its locomotive stock after 1932 when W. A. Stanier had been appointed Chief Mechanical Engineer. *The Economist* had this to say in 1938 about the LMS locomotive policy since the grouping: 'During the last fifteen years as a whole, a virtual revolution has been effected, with the construction of about 3,500 new locomotives. Although many pre-1923 locomotive types (mostly of Midland design) are still regarded as standard, there has been a wholesale slaughter of locomotives of the constituent railways, especially those of the smaller companies.

'At the time of amalgamation there were no fewer than 393 London Midland and Scottish locomotive types; by 1938 this number had been drastically reduced to about 220 and this is in course of being reduced further to 156.

'Standardisation increases the efficiency of construction and repair shops, for it enables the time necessary for repairs to be reduced from weeks to days. Since 1923 the London Midland and Scottish locomotive stock has fallen by over 2,500 units. The number of units under or awaiting repair at the end of 1937 was but one-fifth the number in 1923, but the train mileage was considerably greater, and the average speed of passenger trains had increased; while coal consumption between 1923 and 1937 had fallen by several pounds per locomotive mile, and lubricating oil consumption had been progressively reduced. Expenditure per train mile had fallen, the average wagon load had increased and the number of engine miles per day had risen from well under 100 in 1923 to nearly 120 in 1937.'[23]

By reducing the cost of repairs and renewals, the changes in workshop practice introduced on the LMS reduced the annual financial renewals provision as well as actual expenditure charged to the renewals funds, compared with what would have been required for the original stock of 25 per cent more locomotives than were needed at the end of the period. It would surely be unrealistic to call this 'disinvestment'.

The substantial fall in the total number of locomotives was achieved by more intensive and efficient utilisation – again not 'disinvestment' in any real sense.

Similarly, in the carriage building programmes costs were reduced by standardisation and improved workshop practice, whilst the numbers in the stock were also reduced by higher utilisation.

Only perhaps on the LNER did financial stringency impose limitations on locomotive and carriage building programmes which partly offset the net 'investment' shown by the other grouped companies. Even here there was refreshment of the locomotive types required for the most important duties – express passenger and heavy freight – with 'cascading' of the older engines to lighter duties. Even if the average age of the locomotive stock overall rose, it must be remembered that the steam locomotive is essentially a robust and simple piece of machinery which with proper maintenance including boiler renewals has an almost indefinite life if it is not worked very hard. In such circumstances it may be more economic to maintain older locomotives on secondary duties than to replace them.

The problem of assessing what is and what is not 'investment' is illustrated in the Southern Railway's electrification schemes. Their cost, under Sir Herbert Walker's close supervision, was kept to a minimum in order to avoid swelling the capital expenditure account and possibly creating a need to obtain capital receipts from borrowing or a share issue. One example of the economies practised is the well known case of the provision of new electric passenger carriages by mounting two former steam-hauled six-wheeled carriage bodies on a new steel underframe and bogies. No 'frills' were attached to the scheme – for example, gas lighting at stations on newly electrified lines was not usually replaced by electric light. Such measures helped to ensure that a satisfactory financial return was secured on the outlay. Can one criticise the railway for a failure to 'invest' sufficiently?

It does seem – as Feinstein implicitly recognises – that general statements as to whether or not there was real 'investment' or 'disinvestment' by the main-line railways between 1923 and the outbreak of war are not of great value. One may feel that the subjective opinions of those with personal experience of railway management in the period may have at least as much validity.

Comments on the state of the physical assets yielded varying pictures. The Great Western, as mentioned above, was given high marks. 'Rolling stock was maintained to a very high standard. Injections of new stock were frequent under the standardisation programme. The maintenance of track was of a very high quality – that has always been a Great Western tradition – and it was well maintained in the years up to the war . . . The Chief Engineer of each company was, under the Railway Companies Accounts and Returns Act, required to give a certificate. This perhaps became an anachronism after nationalisation but the auditors did pay considerable attention to the certificate given each year by the Chief Civil Engineer about the state in which the track was maintained. The Western – this is quite a small point – set aside more than adequate funds for the renewal of rolling stock. For example, renewal provisions were continued on stock which was life-expired. When financial stringency became rather acute in the depression years immediately before the war, the policy was altered, but only towards the very end of the period.'[24]

The Southern also was considered largely exempt from criticism because of the marked improvements introduced with electrification, the energetic programme of station reconstruction and the passenger carriage building programmes. Of course, another factor was the relatively lower standard on certain sections at the grouping, which reinforced the claims that the Southern, by and large, improved the condition of the assets it had acquired in 1923. This even applied in outposts such as the Isle of Wight railways, which were greatly strengthened by additional rolling stock and physical improvements.

Accordingly it was primarily the LNER and the LMS over which a question hung. The auditors of the LNER, it was recalled, 'in the last years before the war had to qualify their certificate because of the inadequate financial provision for maintenance'.[25]

Former LNER officers agreed that it 'had to try and skimp and save money'[26] (p. 85), though on the other hand 'all the things that were important for the safe and efficient running of our services were well maintained, and it was no part of the LNER's policy to be slack in that in any regard'.[27] It was in fact rather in rolling stock than permanent way and structures that shabbiness was admitted. 'The shabbiest stock of all was the London end of the LNER . . . the London suburban services . . . and the Great Northern fell a long way behind the standards that were acceptable.'[28] It was emphasised by the same officer that the track was well maintained and safe for high speed and that locomotive shopping was maintained to a reasonable standard. On track maintenance it was insisted that 'the standard was kept up very well there. After all, I think it was in the 1930s when *Mallard* was able to make, and hold, the world record for steam traction of 126 m.p.h. For that you need a first-class track.'[29]

If the essentials were attended to on the LNER, the need for economy was pressing. 'One of the things that we pursued with great vigour, because it was a tremendous field for economy, was extending the period between heavy maintenance in things like paintwork. We did fall behind in the appearance of our premises. We did fall behind in the appearance of our secondary and tertiary passenger services rolling stock, but this is not to suggest for a moment that we fell behind in our standards of anything that mattered to the running efficiency of the system. But we did get more of a run-down look because of this extension of the periods between maintenance.'[30]

The largest question mark hangs over the LMS – not merely was it the largest company but it was the one that devoted most management attention to the introduction of modern business methods. It had a New Works and Parliamentary section at headquarters that scrutinised very closely all proposals for capital expenditure – so closely as to exert what some people described as 'a rather baleful influence on development . . . It used to be regarded as one of the hurdles and I remember the engineering officers and chief officers in the LMS Railway groaning to one another about this.'[31] But it was stressed that in all investment proposals, 'as a purely commercial company, the LMS Railway . . . had to look at things in hard, cold financial terms.'[32]

But it was argued that 'for all that, the system was not that badly maintained. Certainly there was nothing quite as frightful as the conditions into which some of the post-war stations have deteriorated . . . I got around the system quite a lot, and it was my impression that the conditions locally then were not too bad. There had been some deterioration; after all, the terms of trade had moved against the railways very substantially in the 1920s and particularly in the 1930s.'[33]

On the whole, maintenance, it was argued, was better than it has been since the 1939–45 war. 'There was a much greater amount of cleanliness, spit and polish, devoted to a place like Euston. The layout of Euston was very bad . . . On the other hand it was tolerable, given that it was reasonably well maintained. What is tragic is to see sometimes now brand-new good stations created and the slums into which they are allowed to develop, which ruin the whole intention of the exercise.'[34]

The LMS certainly 'from 1931 onwards . . . recognised the need to intensify the use of assets, to intensify the productivity of assets, to produce fewer and more modern equipment assets and, in particular, to improve the commercial services of the company.'[35] This, it seemed, was not incompatible with a certain shabbiness and neglect at the periphery of the business.

The general trend of the subjective comments appears to be that both the Great Western and the Southern, whilst pursuing very different policies, preserved their physical assets well. Where there was some running down it was on the LMS and the LNER; not on the track or on the principal structures, but rather on sectors such as the London suburban services of the LNER and the North London line of the LMS. Overall 'disinvestment', however, seems difficult to prove either by statistics or subjective judgement.

One can only sum up by suggesting that a Scottish verdict of 'not proven' may be applied to the three propositions emerging from Feinstein's work. The first, that there was overall disinvestment between 1920 and 1938, seems doubtful, owing to the unsatisfactory nature of the financial data available. Of course, the position had changed during the war years of 1914–18 and it is certain that intensive user and reduced maintenance must have had a serious adverse effect over that period. But peacetime railway policy, except possibly on the LNER, does not seem to have produced overall 'disinvestment'.

On the second, that the root cause of overall disinvestment was to be found in the 'permanent way and works', equal doubt must apply. Permanent way in the strict sense of track was certainly well maintained. Structures were maintained with full regard for safety, but appearances may have suffered from economies upon superficial maintenance such as station painting programmes.

The last proposition, that there *was* net investment in traction and rolling stock, appears likely to be correct but on other grounds than a methodology which relies solely upon the railway financial returns.

Notes

1 C. Hamilton Ellis, *London Midland and Scottish*, 1970, p. 44.
2 C. Hamilton Ellis, *British Railway History*, vol. II, 1959, p. 329.
3 A. W. Tait (GWR).
4 P. S. Bagwell, *The Transport Revolution from 1770*, 1974, p. 255.
5 Railway Research Service, *The Main Line Railways of Great Britain, 1923–37*, 1938, p. 7.
6 D. H. Aldcroft, *British Railways in Transition*, 1968, p. 69.
7 *Ibid.*, table 10, p. 70; reproduced by courtesy of Macmillan & Co. Ltd.
8 Aldcroft, *British Railways in Transition*, p. 69.
9 *Ibid.*, p. 71.
10 Feinstein, *Domestic Capital Formation in the United Kingdom, 1920–38*, 1965, p. 147.
11 *Ibid.*, p. 153.
12 *Ibid.*, appendix 1.1, p. 8.
13 *Ibid.*, p. 153.
14 *Ibid.*, p. 150.
15 W. Brown, Chief Accountant and later Assistant General Manager, London Midland Region, BR.
16 The most profitable activity of this branch (the track of which was lifted and sent to France in the 1914–18 war but subsequently reinstated) was probably its use by film companies for scenes in *The Wrecker* and *Oh, Mr Porter.*
17 Aldcroft, *British Railways in Transition*, p. 71.

18 But see the reservation made regarding the LNER, p. 89.
19 M. A. Cameron (LNER).
20 *Ibid.*
21 LMS, *A Record of Large-scale Organisation and Management, 1923–46*, 1946, p. 3.
22 *Ibid.*, p. 2.
23 *The Economist* special supplement, 'The L.M.S. Railway', 31 August 1938, p. 12.
24 A. W. Tait (GWR).
25 *Ibid.*
26 M. A. Cameron (LNER).
27 A. R. Dunbar (LNER).
28 *Ibid.*
29 M. A. Cameron (LNER).
30 A. R. Dunbar (LNER).
31 P. E. Garbutt (LMS).
32 *Ibid.*
33 *Ibid.*
34 *Ibid.*
35 D. S. M. Barrie (LMS).

6

The railways and road transport

Early in the motor age several railways obtained road powers, notably the Great Western and the North Eastern. The Great Western used them to operate bus services, notably that from Helston to the Lizard, initiated in 1903; the North Eastern allowed its powers to atrophy because 'the NER under the management of Sir Alexander Butterworth, who hated motors of any description, allowed its road transport activities to decay'.[1] A few services were operated by other railways without statutory powers, apparently unchallenged.

But the Railways Act, 1921, contained no such powers for the new grouped companies; accordingly, the main line railways in 1928 obtained powers to own and operate road transport. The powers were given by four identically worded private Acts, one for each company. The key words in each Act were the powers 'to provide, own, work and use road vehicles to be drawn by animal, electrical or mechanical power in any district to which access is afforded by the system of the Company'.

The new powers were exercised differently in the passenger and the freight fields. The most energetic and prompt steps were taken on the road passenger side, where agreements were made in the first instance with municipal bus operators for joint ownership and working (Caerphilly with the GWR being the first example), and secondly by agreements with the British Electric Traction, Tilling and Scottish Motor Traction groups for railway purchase of substantial interests in all the major bus companies contained within those groups.

By 1931 the four companies had acquired interests in bus companies operating 19,500 vehicles out of a total of 41,500 buses owned by all classes of operator on British roads. Their total investment in bus companies, which had been nil in 1928, had risen in three years to £9,594,111. This was admittedly trifling in relation to the aggregate of past investment in the railway proper, but it was very substantial in relation to total new investment by the companies during those three years.

A critical comment on this process comes from Hibbs: 'The railways displayed this almost feverish activity of acquisition and control partly to protect themselves from road competition and, to a lesser extent, with the aim of "co-ordinating" road and rail services.'[2]

But it should be noted that, in accordance with an undertaking given when the Road Powers Acts were before Parliament, the railways refrained from seeking a controlling interest through their investments, which most commonly comprised either 50 per cent or 49 per cent of the equity. This was done to allay fears that the railways were planning to obtain a monopoly of public road passenger transport.

It should also be remembered that the main-line railways (with the exception of the Southern) had inherited a small number of bus services operated by the pre-grouping companies. The vehicles thus owned in 1923 had amounted to:

LMS	5
LNER	58
GWR	95
SR	1
Total	159

By 1929 the numbers had risen modestly, to:

LMS	54
LNER	77
GWR	108
Total	239

But by 1937 the picture had changed. Practically all the railway passenger road vehicles had been transferred to the rail-associated bus companies. Only the LMS and the LNER together retained a total of 168 vehicles, and these represented the railways' proportionate ownership in the fleets jointly owned with certain municipalities, principally Sheffield and Halifax, managed by Joint Omnibus Committees. The Great Western, which had been almost the first motor bus operator in Great Britain, transferred its last buses in 1933.

In freight, matters progressed much more slowly, largely because the road haulage industry was mainly composed of small, individualistic operators. The railways, however, by a joint purchase obtained full control of two important road transport businesses with which they had in fact long been associated, Carter Paterson and (through the acquisition of the Hay's Wharf Cartage Company) Pickford's.

A 50 per cent interest in Wordie & Co., the railway's cartage agent in Scotland, was acquired by the LMS. Other railway cartage associates that were purchased included Mutter Howey, also in Scotland, and Currie & Co., whilst a 50 per cent interest was acquired in Sutton & Co. There was a cautious move into general road haulage with the acquisition of Joseph Nall & Co., Norman E. Box and a few other firms. Of course, these acquisitions were additional to the railways' existing direct ownership of around 10,000 motor freight vehicles (and some 25,000 horse-drawn vehicles) in 1938, used in their road collection and delivery work. But in view of the total number of goods motor vehicles on the roads, the prospect of a railway monopoly was still very remote. Barker and Savage point out that 'in 1938 there were 228,000 operators (239,000 licence holders) of about 500,000 road goods vehicles of all kind in the country. About 27,000 licence holders owning 93,000 vehicles (of which the railways owned 11 per cent) [10,230] were engaged exclusively in the haulage business.'[3]

There is a further point, that the replacement of horses by motors was proceeding more slowly on the goods side of the road transport industry than on the passenger side, where it had long been complete.

Even so, the railway policies were subject to a good deal of criticism. As early as 1931 the Royal Commission on Transport commented that 'the chief method adopted by the railway companies to protect themselves against road competitors appears to be to "get on the road" themselves'.[4]

The Royal Commission went on: 'In so far as this policy makes for the better co-ordination of rail and road services we welcome it. On the general principle of the policy, however, we cannot refrain from expressing a feeling of doubt whether it is wise for the companies to expend large capital sums for the purpose of establishing services which may be in direct competition with their business as railways. We feel that possibly such capital would be better applied to the electrification of their suburban lines.'[5]

Bagwell is one of several historians who echo this view. 'Their wisdom in taking these steps is questionable. They did not effectively control the policies of the bus companies in which they acquired an interest and although the goods vehicles were used more directly as feeders to the railway, the £15 million invested in the two forms of road transport might have brought in a better return if it had been invested in further schemes for electrification of lines.'[6]

Aldcroft also repeats the Royal Commission's argument, suggesting 'that this money would have been better employed in improving railway facilities proper'.[7] He does agree that the railways' entry into the road transport business 'eventually produced a greater degree of co-ordination between road and rail services, especially on the passenger side' but considers that 'the railways rarely held sufficient shares in the associated companies to give them the power to determine the policy of these concerns to their own advantage'.[8]

On this latter argument, it was pointed out by D. N. (Sir Norman) Chester in 1936 that 'there are two methods by which a co-ordination of road and rail services may be discussed. For each company in which the railway has equal financial interest with the combine group there is a standing joint committee . . . of four members: two from the omnibus side (including the Manager) and two from the railway side. The railway representatives are usually the area commercial officer and a road transport officer from the railway headquarters; where two railways are interested in the company then each has one representative on the committee. The function of this committee is to consider and recommend measures . . . including the running of omnibus services in connection with railway stations and facilities to travel partly by road and partly by rail. The committee is also required to make proposals for developing the traffic of the area generally and to consider proposals for new omnibus services.

'Besides the standing joint committee the railway company also has representation on the omnibus company's board of directors. For example in the case of the Eastern, Southern and Western National Omnibus Companies, the railway company and the Tilling group . . . may each nominate half the board so long as each, or either, hold 50 per cent of the issued ordinary shares.'[9]

On the face of it, such arrangements should have promoted a useful degree of co-ordination. A transport authority, C. T. Brunner,[10] claimed that the road powers Acts constituted 'the first official admission that its rival, the motor transport industry, is more efficient for certain purposes than the railways and we may expect that, if the railways do not use their powers unfairly to strangle road competition, which in any case would be an extremely difficult task today, it will result in a further transference of traffic from rail to road, albeit in railway-owned road vehicles. The railways are apparently trying to solve their problem . . . by changing from railway companies to general operators of transport services.'[11] But Brunner felt that there were 'grave dangers to the public in allowing the railways to run road services except under careful supervision . . . railway managers . . . are not likely to explore the possibilities of road transport with anything like the same enthusiasm as people interested primarily in the subject'.[12]

This fear of monopoly contrasts with the opposite criticism that the railway investments in bus companies made insufficient difference to bus policy. However, the latter criticism was repeated in the second reading debate on the Transport Bill, 1946, by Douglas Jay (Labour, Battersea North). 'Railways,' he argued, 'have come into a virtual private monopoly with road transport during the last fifteen years. Although the railways were given power to run road vehicles in 1928, they made very little use of that power but instead bought up controlling shares [*sic*] in virtually all the private bus companies in the country.' The wild inaccuracies in this statement are obvious; they were promptly challenged by the Railway Companies' Association.

A contrary view was also strongly argued by the LMS in the same year, 1946, to the effect that, in the circumstances of 1928, investment in established undertakings had been essential; however, 'had success in obtaining road powers been achieved earlier, inter-relationship of rail and road traffic might have been effected, but in the circumstances then obtaining it became necessary to co-operate with established road undertakings, rather than embark on the costly alternative of providing large fleets of omnibuses and lorries.'[13] The implication of this rather cryptic remark seems to be that it was cheaper to buy a half-share in well-established businesses than to set up in competition with them; and that in 1928, anyway, funds for the latter were no longer available.

It was strongly claimed that 'this new relationship between the railway and the omnibus undertakings enabled matters of common interest to be brought regularly under review with mutual benefit. It was possible to correlate the services offered by both forms of passenger transport through an adjustment of timings to give improved rail and bus connections, by making tickets available by either form, and by arranging bus services as feeders for rail excursions or road services as feeders of rail excursions. It was also found possible to withdraw unremunerative passenger services on branch lines by arranging with the associated omnibus company to provide or adjust its services to meet the needs of the public.'[14] Later critics have argued that the policy of replacing little-used rail services with buses was totally inadequate, though the LMS pointed to the achievement of other forms of co-ordination.

'By 1939, the vehicles of associated bus companies served over 1,000 L.M.S. stations by using the station forecourt, stopping at or adjacent to the station or by being available within 200 yards. In the previous year 541,000 bus or rail tickets were used on return journeys for bus or rail travel.'[15]

Rather less glowing accounts were given by railway officers thirty years later. 'The policy as I remember it was to go into partnership with bus operators and provide up to 50 per cent of the capital, and leave the running of the services to the bus professionals, with a policy committee guiding them about the services on which they should concentrate and so on . . . in the period between the wars I didn't feel it was the kind of thing that mattered nearly as much as concentrating on the improvement of our rail services.'[16] Such a view supports the criticism voiced by the Royal Commission and Aldcroft; but it is not unchallenged. A different LNER argument criticised the concentration upon purely railway operations. 'It is just not true that the railway companies failed to foresee the future of road transport. Some of their officers foresaw it very clearly, but they were overridden by "superiors" who were obsessed with other priorities, which was a very great pity.'[17] Company discipline apparently inhibited many of the younger officers from expressing publicly views contrary to those of their superiors.

It was also argued that individual railway officers on the Standing Joint Committees tried to promote co-ordination and prevent 'such stupid things as the erection of a bus station in Darlington a good ten minutes' walk away from the railway station'.[18] The railway officers had made 'strenuous efforts to avoid the sort of nonsense I have mentioned at Darlington, but they were unsuccessful'.[19]

There is an interesting question whether it was principally the attitude of management or that of the unions which made it difficult for the railways to exploit their road passenger investments in the direction of fuller road–rail co-ordination. Complications there certainly were over union membership; the early GWR buses had been staffed by members of the National Union of Railwaymen – a fact viewed with disfavour by the Transport and General Workers' Union. Railway and bus company pay scales, of course, differed.

A Great Western view was as follows. 'Having pioneered both haulage and bus services in the earliest days, the GWR fell into line with the policy of the four main-line companies, which was to exercise a measure of control by setting up what, I suppose, amounted to a transport conglomerate . . . management of the concerns taken over . . . was left very much to the undertakings, subject to a detailed annual review of both policies and finances. . . . in the case of the bus companies, formal standing committees of local officers produced a degree of co-ordination of local arrangements on fares, services and proceedings in the licensing courts. . . . one of the things which has always bedevilled transport co-ordination is the opposition of the Transport and General Workers' Union and the railway unions. . . . this may have been one of the difficulties . . . far more than any antagonism between managements.'[20]

The question whether the railways should or should not run bus services themselves was certainly given a good deal of thought. 'Don't infer that Walker – I talked this over with Wedgwood on several occasions and with Milne – the general managers themselves were totally against having a direct control. Walker put it this way: "We are not busmen and we never will be. We want to employ the professionals to run our investment. If we start putting Bushrods and other people (excellent railwaymen) in charge, the thing will fail." '[21]

In consequence, Walker's instructions to his officers representing the Southern Railway on bus company boards were precise. ' "When you go into the Board meetings at Crewe House [Tilling group] and at 88 Kingsway [BET group] you go as a busman, not as a railwayman. I don't want you going there and arguing the railway case. You represent the money we have invested in those bus companies. You are only to oppose bus development on the Southern system if you are convinced that it is unnecessary competition which will rob us of a useful and profitable business that we are already doing. On those occasions you should say, 'I can't agree to that without consultation at Waterloo.' But whatever you do, don't get labelled as a railwayman or they will never give you their confidence."

'That was the mistake that the LMS made, because, with much the biggest investment of us all, they always appeared as railwaymen. All the people in BET from John Wills downwards, and at Tilling's, said the same thing to me. "You got the results you did because of the successful way in which the Southern handled its bus investment." I said, "That was due to the instructions we had from Walker." '[22]

But it did not appear on the Southern that there was a serious clash of interests. 'I was on the Board of the Southern Vectis company, which we bought when Kennedy was chairman. I was on the Board of every company, the East Kent, Maidstone & District, Thames Valley, Southern National, Devon National, Southdown. On no single occasion that I can recall was there a serious difference, after a good discussion at Waterloo with the traffic side, both commercial and operation, which I never failed to do before going to a bus Board. I would take the agenda with me to Cox. "What is your line on this? What do you feel about this?" So I'd briefed myself properly on the railway side.'[23]

The relations of the Southern Railway with the bus companies were perhaps exceptionally good. 'The Southern had the best liaison of the four main-line companies. It was very good, for example, with the Southdown company; it was helped by the fact that the Southern electric train service pattern was based on hourly or half-hourly standard frequencies, and this matched the pattern of bus timetables better than the train services still operated by steam on other railways.'[24]

Another view, from the LNER, was that 'a lot more could have been done if instead of just investing in bus companies the railways had started to run some of their own passenger services by road, which they could have done. But the thing that held them up there was the certainty that if they provided railway-owned passenger services they would immediately be forced by the unions to pay railway rates of pay, which at that stage were higher than what road people were getting.'[25] Once again, union difficulties were adduced.

On the question of co-ordination another fundamental problem was highlighted. 'I was a bus company director, and in general we tried to encourage some sort of timetable co-ordination at stations, but that was obviously an acute difficulty because of the question of punctuality. The railways rather prided themselves on their punctuality. If the bus was held up because more people than usual wanted to use it, do you hold the train or do you not? . . . I cannot remember any clear instructions as to whether we put the bus company first or the railway. I think I naturally would have put the railway first, as far as I could, but knowing that I could not control the thing.'[26]

The much smaller investment in road goods transport, following the grant of statutory powers, has not attracted so much criticism from historians as the bus investments, partly perhaps because they were so much smaller. Brunner had agreed that 'there is undoubtedly a large section of transport work which can best be accomplished by a combination of railway for one part of the journey and road for the other, but if a large part of the road transport passed into the hands of the railway companies, it would certainly tend to strengthen the power of the railway unions and make the position of the general public worse in time of strikes'.[27]

This certainly did not happen. As Aldcroft remarks, the extent of the railways' interest in road haulage 'was too limited to have a really significant effect in curtailing the degree of "outside" competition'.[28]

Some support for Aldcroft's view comes from a former senior railway officer. 'They didn't use the letters patent to go out into road haulage, in a sense to diversify, looking ahead to a general scaling down of railway freight "smalls" operations and expansion of road freight. It doesn't seem to have occurred to them that this would take place. They were concerned about a rearguard action on charges, the "Square Deal", and so on.'[29]

An officer of another railway endorsed this. 'I have always entertained doubts about the policy which was followed by the railway companies in the way they ran their road interests. Sir Ralph Wedgwood himself produced a very thoroughgoing report on road competition in 1930 which led to what followed on the LNER, but in the case of Currie's, which I happen to know rather well because I was very much mixed up with it, there was continued resistance to any expansion by way of making a really big impact upon road haulage in north-east England, because the LNER had not got a controlling interest, and time after time it was quite obvious that Currie & Co., albeit partly owned by the LNER, was solely concerned about the profitability of Currie & Co. They preferred to have a short list of very good reliable customers producing a very nice return on the capital investment, and turned a deaf ear to almost every suggestion of expansion.

'My other comment is that I rather doubt whether it was a wise policy, having acquired Hay's Wharf, with Carter Paterson's, to take the line that that company, having been acquired, should be operated strictly along the lines of that company's interest as such without reference at all to the larger interest of the railway companies owning it. I would much have preferred to have seen a policy of, if you like, forced co-operation, so that there was a co-operative arrangement, very clearly understood, by which the road transport companies owned by the railway companies would become, if you like, subsidiary and servant to the railway companies, whereas in fact they were allowed to compete with them, the grounds being that that was the only way of enabling those companies to compete with the outside operator.'[30]

The real criticism seems to be that a great opportunity presented itself which was not effectively seized. 'Carter Paterson did enter into an arrangement with the LMS company by which "smalls" traffic was carried by railway as a trunk haul from Manchester to London. But the example was never adequately followed up.'[31]

Perhaps the really significant result of the railway investment in road haulage was the fear that it might be greatly extended, which undoubtedly produced the 'concordat' during the 'Square Deal' campaign in 1938–39 and the Road–Rail Agreement of 1946 which was intended to demonstrate that the intended nationalisation was irrelevant, since voluntary agreements on services and rates could be achieved under continuing private ownership.

This agreement, set out in a memorandum of principles submitted jointly by the main-line railways and the Road Haulage Association to the Minister of Transport, falls outside the period covered by this study. It was dismissed by the government as leading to the creation of a privately owned transport monopoly: its main interest as a historical event is not so much its character of a deathbed repentance as whether or not it was stimulated by the road powers granted to the railways in 1928.

Notes

1 A. A. Harrison (LNER).

2 J. Hibbs, *British Bus Services*, 1968, p. 99.
3 T. C. Barker and C. I. Savage, *An Economic History of Transport in Britain*, 1975, p. 177.
4 Royal Commission on Transport, *Final Report*, (Cmd. 1751) 1931, Summary of Conclusions, p. 151.
5 *Ibid.*
6 P. S. Bagwell, *The Transport Revolution from 1770*, 1974, p. 257.
7 D. H. Aldcroft, *British Railways in Transition*, 1968, p. 86.
8 *Ibid.*
9 D. N. Chester, *Public Control of Road Passenger Transport*, Manchester University Press, 1936, p. 41.
10 Christopher T. Brunner, CBE, 1903–62. Author of *The Problems of Motor Transport*, *Road versus Rail*, *The Problem of Oil*. Head of Statistical Department, Shell-Mex & BP, 1927. Later a Managing Director, Shell-Mex & BP. President of the Institute of Transport, 1951.
11 C. T. Brunner, *Road versus Rail*, 1929, p. 71.
12 *Ibid.*, p. 72.
13 LMS, *A Record of Large-scale Organisation and Management, 1923–46*, 1946, p. 18.
14 *Ibid.*
15 *Ibid.*
16 A. R. Dunbar (LNER).
17 A. A. Harrison (LNER).
18 *Ibid.*
19 *Ibid.*
20 A. W. Tait (GWR).
21 Sir John Elliot (SR).
22 *Ibid.*
23 *Ibid.*
24 J. L. Harrington (SR).
25 M. A. Cameron (LNER).
26 *Ibid.*
27 *Road versus Rail*, p. 74.
28 Aldcroft, *British Transport since 1914*, p. 335.
29 D. S. M. Barrie (LMS).
30 A. A. Harrison (LNER).
31 *Ibid.*

7

The railways and air transport

Not a great deal has been written about the railways' involvement with air transport between 1933 and 1939.[1] It may be noted that the background to their move into airline operation was very different from that in the road transport industry at the same period. Road transport was well established by 1928, when the railways' road powers were obtained. By and large, it was profitable and, especially on the passenger side, there were large undertakings with a good record of financial stability. In air transport things were very different. Although many air-minded pioneers were convinced that civil aviation must have a bright future, the technology for commercial exploitation was still inadequate. Quite simply, the planes of the 1920s were too slow and unreliable, their seating capacity was much too small, and they lacked the navigational aids to enable them to fly at night or in bad weather. Imperial Airways' four-engined biplane, the HP42, had a cruising speed of 100 m.p.h. and seats for thirty-eight passengers – and it was the pride of the fleet!

With speeds so low, the advantage over surface transport was not very great. And with a service very much at the mercy of weather conditions, and restricted to daytime operation, it is not surprising that very low load factors were experienced. The annual collapse of traffic during the winter months meant that many services found it necessary to operate only during the summer, with substantial overhead costs accruing during the winter.

In such circumstances losses were almost inevitable except on a few routes where a circuitous surface journey could be shortened by an air 'hop'. Even the premier traffic route, London–Paris, was economically shaky. The result was a mushrooming of companies which opened routes, changed them, closed them and then either disappeared or merged with another airline.

Survival and growth depended upon external financial support. This might come if an airline was a minor activity within a large financial conglomerate such as Whitehall Securities; alternatively, government aid might be forthcoming either as a direct subsidy or as a concealed one through high payments for the carriage of mails, as in the USA.

In Britain, Imperial Airways was the 'flag carrier', supported for strategic and prestige reasons much as the German government supported Deutsche Lufthansa, founded in 1926. After the railways began to involve themselves, although the mushroom growth and disappearance of small airlines continued, there were two important underlying factors: the move towards the all-metal monoplane and higher seating capacity coupled with better operational characteristics; and the support given by governments to the growth of a national airline, or possibly two airlines, one providing international flights and one domestic. By 1939 matters had changed so much that in the summer of that year Air France was advertising a service between London (Croydon) and Paris (Le Bourget) 'every hour, on the hour' throughout the day. Admittedly it was short-lived, being replaced by a joint Air France/Imperial Airways service; but it demonstrates how far the airlines had come in the previous decade.

This, then, was the field which the railways cautiously entered. The necessary powers were obtained, a year after the 1928 road powers, by four short, almost identically worded Acts of Parliament, with eight clauses giving power to own and operate air services within the territory served by each company and also the London area (actually the Metropolitan Police District) and (a noteworthy addition) in Europe as far as longitude 20° E, which excluded the USSR and most of eastern Europe.

Another similarity with the exercise of the road powers was the joint partnership between the railways and established airline operators, through this was by no means as straightforward or standardised as in the case of the bus companies.

Here the similarities end. And on the other hand the disimilarities with the road transport investment were striking. First of all, the air transport investments were mostly unprofitable, in marked contrast to the road transport holdings. Secondly, the policies of the companies diverged considerably. The LNER was comparatively little involved, for two reasons. For a long time no internal air services were started by private operators which competed significantly with that railway's major traffic routes such as the East Coast main line or the London–West Riding business trains; and the company had far less disposable cash resources for investment than the three others.

The other companies all showed considerable interest, but – again in contrast to their actions over road transport – they were in no hurry to exercise the powers they obtained when their Bills passed into law on 10 May 1929. In fact they waited over four years before entering the field at all effectively. A major factor was probably the degree and nature of personal interest in air transport shown by the railway chief executives. Sir Josiah Stamp of the LMS was interested in the principle of railway access to a competitive activity, but he delegated active participation to his Vice-President for Research, Sir Harold Hartley. Perhaps the earliest real interest in air had been shown by Sir Felix Pole of the GWR, but he left the railway in 1929. However, his successor, Sir James Milne, was apparently also attracted by the commercial and prestige value of a railway airline and his Assistant General Manager, K. W. C. Grand,[2] was very active on behalf of the Great Western.

The Southern had for some time watched the growth of Continental air traffic, especially between London and Paris, and Sir Herbert Walker seems to have shared the view that the railway must not be excluded from participating. He entrusted the main work of developing the Southern Railway interest to J. B. (later Sir John) Elliot, Assistant Traffic Manager and later Assistant General Manager; and also to J. L. Harrington,[3] for a time a member of Walker's personal staff.

The Southern was the first company to make a move, by purchasing a substantial number of shares in Imperial Airways which, however, failed to provide a controlling interest. The Imperial Airways holding was therefore soon sold, in 1929, and was followed by inconclusive discussions on rail–air co-operation which did not get very far.

The first effective railway air service was started by the Great Western in April 1933, using aircraft and staff provided by Imperial Airways on the GWR's behalf on the Birmingham–Cardiff–Plymouth route. A year later the four railways combined to form Railway Air Services Ltd, with a capital of £50,000 and participation by Imperial Airways and (later) Coast Lines Ltd. Sir Harold Hartley of the LMS was chairman, and the LMS played a major role in RAS policy, the basis of which was operation of particular routes on behalf of an individual sponsoring railway company which accepted financial responsibility for the service. Technical services were provided for RAS by Imperial Airways.

From the start, most RAS services were operated for the LMS and GWR. By 1939 these included the 'backbone' routes of London (Croydon) to Glasgow via Birmingham, Liverpool and Belfast; also London to Glasgow via Manchester. But the picture is one of numerous services being started, changed and abandoned at short notice. At various times Plymouth–Birmingham–Liverpool, Leeds/Bradford to the Isle of Man, Cardiff–Bristol, etc., were operated, usually in the summer only.

The picture is also complicated by the number of non-RAS services sponsored by the railways in association with small independent air operators. Spartan Airlines Ltd – a subsidiary company of the Saunders–Roe aircraft manufacturing firm in the Isle of Wight – was associated with the Southern Railway in operating services to the Island from, successively, the Croydon, Heston and Gatwick aerodromes.

The LMS also operated (with the Isle of Man Steam Packet Company) a non-RAS service to the Isle of Man for a while in 1935, in which the Olley aviation group later joined. The GWR and the SR jointly took a half-share in one of the few profitable ventures, Channel Islands Airways Ltd, in 1939.

In 1939 air transport to the Orkneys and Shetlands and the Western Isles of Scotland was strengthened by the setting up of Scottish Airways Ltd, in which the LMS had a 40 per cent interest.

This short and incomplete account is nevertheless sufficient to show the complex and varied character of the railways' involvement in air transport up to 1939, partly through services provided by Railway Air Services Ltd and partly through *ad hoc* (and not very durable) arrangements with other operators. The complexity is well illustrated by the accompanying diagram, showing the organisation and financial interests in 1939, in which the Pearson financial group, Whitehall Securities Ltd, had participated since the mid-1930s. The full picture of the Whitehall Securities, Olley and railway interests in air transport is even more complex, but this abbreviated diagram of the early associations illustrates the scope of the involvement.

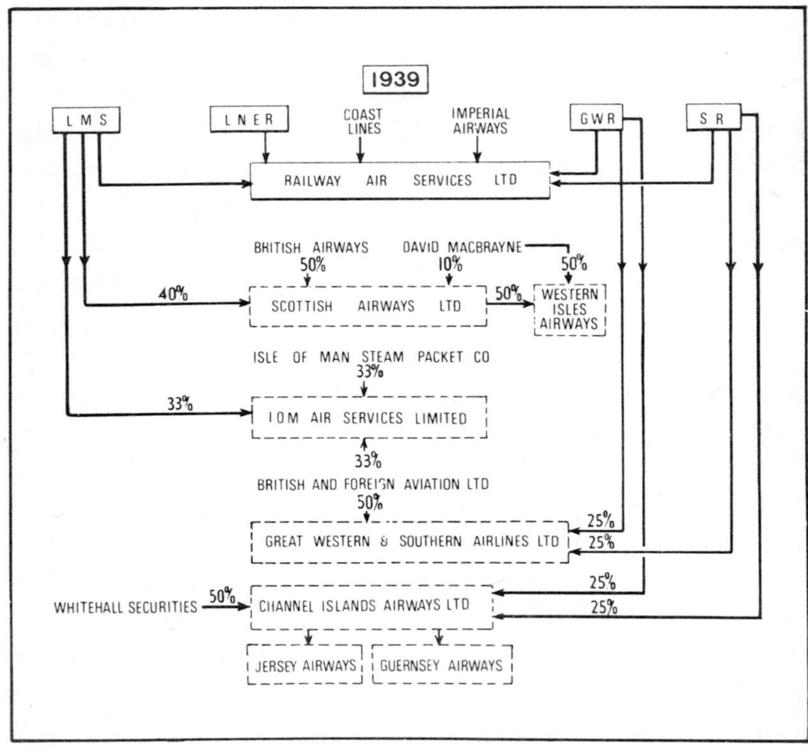

Before considering the criticisms that have been made of the railways' policy, it is necessary to repeat that most of their ventures into air transport had – like most airline operations between the wars – lost money. J. N. Faulkner points out that 'during the five complete years 1934–38 the railways had lost £195,000 on their air services in relation to a revenue of only £100,000. While the LMS had lost the largest sum, in proportion to turnover, it had done better on its trunk routes than the GWR and SR, who had sponsored seasonal, and often devious, services which seem to have been conceived as aerial versions of traditional cross-country trains.'[4]

The LMS, arguing in 1946 the case against railway nationalisation, took pride in its air transport record. 'An important part was played in the development of civil aviation on routes related to L.M.S. surface interests. As journeys involving sea passages were most promising, services were instituted between London, Birmingham, Liverpool, Manchester and Belfast; Glasgow and Belfast; Lancashire and the Isle of Man and in Scotland. These activities in air transport were conducted in co-operation with other shipping interests and co-ordination was effected with other operators.

'The public benefits from the co-ordination of rail and air transport included interchange of air and rail tickets, conveyance of luggage by rail for air passengers, and the use of railway stations and town offices for air bookings and seat reservations.

'The associated air services were in 1938 flying some 2,000,000 miles, carrying 40,000 passengers and 1,500,000 pounds of mails and freight.'[5]

The powers to operate air services to the Continent were not exercised for some time, but in 1938 the GWR- and SR-sponsored routes of Railway Air Services were linked up with an Olley company, Channel Air Ferries Ltd, which had services to the Scilly Isles, Le Touquet, Deauville and Luxembourg. This was, however, far from giving the Southern Railway the major share in the prime Continental services to Paris and Brussels, which might have seemed a logical development and which the Southern had sought to obtain through its purchase of Imperial Airways shares.

As mentioned earlier, criticism of the railways' policy in the air has been fairly restrained, and this may be partly due to the complex nature of the various ventures with which the companies were associated, and to the relatively minor volume of traffic handled in comparison with that passing by traditional surface transport. Aldcroft points out that railway participation in air transport has been criticised because the railway companies were merely furthering or protecting their own interests.[6] (However, since the railways were in private ownership, accountable to their shareholders, this can scarcely rate as a major criticism.)

Aldcroft continues, 'There can be no doubt that the entry of the railways into air transport was determined by outside developments in the field. They had obtained air transport powers in 1929 but made no attempt to use them until the establishment of internal air services by private operators in the early 1930s appeared to threaten their own interests.'[7] Early in 1934 Sir Josiah Stamp made it clear that the railways were not going to sit back and let the airlines rob them of their traffic. 'The matter,' he said, 'has assumed some urgency with us, owing to the more recent activities of certain established airway companies and their preparations for the inauguration of regular commercial services between important centres in competition with our rail services. It is desirable for the four main-line companies to act in co-operation.'[8] The railways were obviously determined not to make the same mistake they had made with road transport in the 1920s, when they had allowed the new competitor to establish a strong foothold before participating themselves. Indeed, the railways themselves admitted that the main reason for the promotion of the Railway (Air Transport) Bills in 1928–29 was so that they might be 'at liberty to take a share in the inevitable development of air transport and avoid a repetition of their experience in regard to road transport'. As the journal of air transport, *Flight*, remarked somewhat later, 'the railway companies, still sore from their battle with road transport, are prepared to fight any rivalry from the air'.[9]

Aldcroft is inclined to agree that 'apart from one or two cases, notably Midland & Scottish Air Ferries and possibly North Eastern Airways, there appears to be little evidence to confirm the belief that the railways deliberately tried to strangle private operators. On the other hand they did endeavour to gain control by acquiring a financial interest in private air companies, and eventually only a few remained outside the railway grouping. . . . There is no doubt that railway participation brought about a reduction of competition through a rationalisation of services. By allocating routes to various companies a certain amount of duplication was avoided. But this was by no means a bad thing.'[10]

He concludes that on balance the railways made 'a significant contribution to the development of air transport. Though they had secured a semi-monopoly of air transport services within Great Britain by the late 1930s it would be wrong to suggest that they openly abused their favourable position. Nevertheless the attitude of the railways was far from impartial and, as we have seen, policy was often determined by a consideration of their own interests.'[11]

R. E. G. Davies gives some guarded praise. 'The Great Western, Southern, and London, Midland and Scottish Railways all played a part in the development of trunk services in the United Kingdom. Though the development of these services can hardly be described as enthusiastic or severely competitive – such competition would have been against their own interests – the railways brought to British air transport the stability and organization vitally necessary for the establishment of regular trunk services, in contrast to seasonal holiday flights run by some of the smaller independents.'[12] He also stresses that some of the railway-associated air services were both commercially successful and technically efficient. 'The railways progressively increased their holding in Channel Islands Airways until the company and its subsidiaries were wholly owned by them.

'The services of Jersey Airways were immensely popular. Traffic was consistently high during the summer holiday season, building up to a figure of 34,000 in 1938. Always patrons of de Havilland equipment, the airline became the first operators of the seventeen-seater high-wing DH 95 Flamingo when this aircraft, de Havilland's first all-metal airliner, went into service experimentally in July 1939, cutting the London–Jersey time to one hour . . .

'Railway Air Services thus served, by their trunk routes and those of their subsidiary companies, the entire United Kingdom, on a network which stretched from Jersey to the Shetland Islands. In providing a service to the far north of Scotland, however, they had a vigorous rival, an independent service provided by a combination of Aberdeen Airways, formed by E. L. Gandar Dower in January 1934, and North Eastern Airways, formed early in 1935.'[13]

North Eastern Airways incurred the hostility of the LNER with its short-lived London (Heston) to Newcastle service in 1935, later extended to Edinburgh. The LNER attitude may have been a major factor in the 'booking ban', as it was known, under which the railway companies informed their ticket agencies that bookings might not be made for non-railway-associated airlines' internal services without permission from the Railway Clearing House.

A rather severe critic of railway policy is John King, whose two interesting but still unpublished papers,[14] containing much detailed research, also contain some judgements of a subjective character. His main argument is that 'the railways in the inter-war years were behaving as monopolists – and not very enlightened ones at that! The railways entered air transport to control it. 'The framework of the railway airline was nothing more than a front for the restrictionist philosophy of the railways.'[15]

King makes the general point that 'the railways were essentially oligopolists, and this was amply demonstrated in their involvement in air transport . . . there was very little policy disagreement between the railway companies in their air transport involvement. There was certainly no rivalry between the companies and no disagreements on providing joint services between more than one railway's territory.'[16]

King's criticisms are rather more severe than those of most historians. They should perhaps be looked at in the light of the railways' financial position and statutory duties. First of all, by the 1930s the railways had seen quite clearly the extent to which their future was threatened, immediately by road competition and, more distantly and conjecturally, by air transport. Their prime duty was to earn dividends for their proprietors within the statutory framework laid down for them by Parliament. To ignore the possibility of damaging future competition from air would have been neglectful. To assume that rail transport would always be able to compete with air would have been unrealistic. So gaining a foothold in the new form of transport was obviously an appropriate move.

At the same time, their overall financial difficulties precluded laying out large sums in what, on the basis of existing performance, would in most cases have been loss-making activities. It is therefore difficult to see what other course – either refraining from any activity in the air, or alternatively committing very large sums to air transport – could have been justified by the Boards to the shareholders.

However, one critic who had been close to Sir Harold Hartley on the LMS at the time took, perhaps surprisingly, quite a critical view. 'The Railway Air Service was a most curious development. I do not think it was realised at the time – certainly I did not realise it at the time, but I have since seen papers which indicate it fairly clearly – that the basic purpose in setting up Railway Air Services and developing internal air services, railway-owned, in the United Kingdom was to suppress possible competition. It was not for the furtherance of air travel. It was to prevent the railways from losing traffic to some air competitor. They were mainly concerned with getting in on routes, establishing themselves and then operating a holding exercise, a restraining exercise, to stop anybody else from getting in and building up a substantial air traffic.'[17]

Apart from RAS operations, the investment in the small independents was also criticised. 'I think that the British railway companies, the old main-line companies, penetrated quite a few of those independent companies and eventually took them over, or else owned a large slice of the equity by the time they were finished. At the time I did not realise that there was this purpose behind the exercise to stop air competition.'[18]

On the other hand, most 'inside' comment defended the railways' policies, in particular the Southern's desire to participate in the Continental business. 'To go back to Walker and Geddes,[19] what happened was this. The interchange of tickets was something we were very keen on. The bid by the Southern for the valuable air services between London and Paris and London and Brussels failed because Walker and Geddes could not agree on the price. I was there, taking notes. That was all. That was the disagreement: Geddes wanted to be rid of near European services, and to concentrate on world and empire routes. Not on policy.'[20]

The point was also made that the railways fostered a sense of responsibility in air transport, an example being on the service to the Channel Isles. 'There had been a proposal to run a joint Channel Island service, but this had had to wait, on safety and operational grounds, until there was a proper airport in Jersey. The previous service had landed and taken off from the beach, and this was not considered satisfactory by Railway Air Services Ltd.'[21]

The same point was put even more strongly. 'At first we wouldn't take it on. So long as they landed on the sand, we said "No". Keith Grand was very strong on that, and eventually a kid had his head cut off with a propeller. We said, "As soon as you can give us something to land on, we will come." And it became a very successful operation.'[22]

On general commercial grounds too the railway venture was considered justified. 'Let's take, for instance, the route from South Wales. Surely it was extremely logical for the Great Western – once again they were enterprising – to operate services by air through Railway Air Services from Cardiff to Weston-super-Mare and along to the Channel Islands, because were they not doing two things? So far as the Channel Islands were concerned, were they not only defending their own shipping services from erosion by air competitors but also making it possible to be the sitting tenant if the almost total supersession of those steamer services became economically necessary? Where would they have been if they had gone on fighting a rearguard action on those shipping services and then been conquered by some independent airline? Surely it was better to prop them up, to be in on the ground floor? Let us remember that the period over which Railway Air Services operated was extremely limited. It was a field in which the airliner as such was not very far developed. I flew with them. I helped to publicise them. Were they not technically feeling their way as well as commercially?'[23]

The question of criticism made with hindsight also arose. 'I think they have to be judged in the context of the state of air traffic development at that time.'[24]

This remark is perhaps as apposite as any comment on the policy. With internal air services attracting adventurous and air-minded people such as E. L. Gandar Dower, there was a mushroom growth of companies. In some cases they performed very useful services, such as those to the Orkneys and Shetlands, the Western Isles of Scotland, the Isle of Man and above all the Channel Islands, where awkward sea crossings could be eliminated. Others operated on overland routes where, with the slow machines then available, the time saving over rail was not significant enough to abstract much traffic.

Very few of the companies achieved financial viability. Davies lists 'those that fell by the wayside, 1932–39'.[25] They number twelve airlines, very few of which operated any services for more than a year or two.

It seems to be clear that the railway involvement brought in *some* stability. RAS used the best British-made aircraft available, concentrating upon routes which offered the best prospect of future permanent financial viability. At the same time the railways were never in a position to act as complete monopolists, even in RAS, where Imperial Airways and Coast Lines were joint shareholders. And in Sottish Airways the railway interest (LMS) was only 40 per cent; in Isle of Man Air Services (also LMS) only 33 per cent; in Great Western & Southern Airlines (GWR and SR) only 50 per cent; in Channel Islands Airways only 50 per cent. The possibility of a railway stranglehold seems remote.

As a postscript, whilst most internal air services were suspended during the war, at the end of it the railways were poised to resume operations on a large scale and become the dominant internal airline operator, as the Cadman Committee had recommended and the 'caretaker' Conservative government in 1945 was prepared to accept in principle when the future of British European Airways was being considered. This possibility, which was of course scotched by the Labour victory in July 1945, might have given some validity to the criticism that the railways were monopoly-minded – more perhaps than in the inter-war years which are the subject of this study.

Notes

1 Exceptions to this general statement are (1) D. H. Aldcroft, 'The Railways and Air Transport, 1933–39'; a chapter in that author's *Studies in British Transport History, 1870–1970*, 1974; (2) the same author's 'Britain's internal airways, the pioneer stage of the 1930s', *Business History*, June 1964; (3) J. N. Faulkner, 'British railways and civil aviation, 1929–48', *Railway World*, February 1978; (4) two unpublished papers by John King, 'Railway Involvement in Air Transport in the British Isles, 1929–39' and 'Lord Swinton and the Railways'.

2 Keith W. C. Grand, b. 1900. Joined GWR 1919. USA representative, 1926–29. Assistant General Manager, GWR, 1929–47. General Manager (acting) GWR, 1947. Chief Regional Officer, Western Region, BR, 1948–54. General Manager, WR, 1954–59. Member, British Transport Commission, 1959–62. Chairman, Coast Lines, 1968–71.

3 J. L. Harrington, b. 1906. Assistant to Traffic Manager, SR, 1934. Divisional Marine Manager, Dover, 1938. General Assistant to General Manager, 1941. Chief Officer, Adiministration and Marine, BR, 1951. Chief Shipping and International Services Officer, BTC, 1956. General Manager (Shipping and International Services), British Railways Board, 1968. Retired 1971.

4 Faulkner, 'British railways and civil aviation'.

5 LMS, *A Record of Large-scale Organisation and Management, 1923–46*, 1946, p. 19.

6 Aldcroft, 'Britain's internal airways'.

7 *Ibid.*, p. 226.

8 *Report of the Proceedings at the 11th Ordinary General Meeting of the Proprietors of the LMS Railway Company*, 23 February 1934.

9 *Flight*, 1 March 1934, p. 192.

10 'Britain's internal airways', p. 236.

11 *Ibid.*, p. 239.

12 R. E. G. Davies, *A History of the World's Airlines*, 1964, p. 103.

13 *Ibid.*, p. 108. E. L. Gandar Dower, b. *c.* 1909. Actor and sportsman. Founded Allied Airways 1934, Scottish Air Lines and associated companies, 1934–5, British–Norwegian Air Line 1937. Founder, Association of British Aircraft Operators 1944. MP for Caithness and Sutherland, 1945–50.

14 See n. 1 above.

15 J. King, 'Railway involvement in air transport', p. 6.

16 *Ibid.*

17 P. E. Garbutt (LMS).

18 *Ibid.*

19 Rt. Hon. Sir Eric (Campbell) Geddes, PC, GCB, GBE, KCB, 1875–1937. Chief Goods Manager, NER 1907. Deputy General Manager, 1911. Deputy Director General, Munitions Supply, 1915–16. Director General, Transportation, 1916–17. Director General of Military Railways, 1916–17. First Lord of the Admiralty, 1917–18. Minister of Transport, 1919–21. Chairman, Imperial Airways, 1921.

20 Sir John Elliot (SR).

21 J. L. Harrington (SR).

22 Sir John Elliot (SR).

23 D. S. M. Barrie (LMS).

24 *Ibid.*

25 *A History of the World's Airlines*, p. 107.

8

Technical standards and innovation

Most of the criticisms of railway policy in the field of innovation and technical standards fall into two groups. First is the issue of traction policy, and the long adherence to steam at a time when other countries were embarking on major electrification projects and – to a lesser extent – developing the use of diesel power. Then there is the whole question of freight handling methods, in particular the continued use of the small loose-coupled four-wheeled wagon.

This is not to say that passenger services entirely escaped criticism. The absence of a baggage registration system, the delay in providing sleeping accommodation for other than first-class passengers, and above all the quality of certain commuter services, all came under fire from time to time. But, by and large, the serious and sustained criticisms from students of railway policy were confined to the two areas mentioned above.

The criticisms of traction policy vary according to whether they are contemporary, i.e. between the wars, or more recent. Between 1923 and 1939 most writers on railway policy seemed to accept that continued reliance on steam was reasonable, except that electrification of suburban routes was obviously desirable. In this respect the Southern was considered to set an example which other railways, above all the LNER, would have done well to follow. The LNER's former Great Eastern suburban lines from Liverpool Street, and to a lesser extent the Great Northern lines from King's Cross, were the target of much adverse comment. Some railway officers have admitted that it was justified. 'The shabbiest stock of all was the London end of the LNER – the London suburban services . . . and the Great Northern fell a long way behind the standards that were acceptable.'[1] In fact, complaints about these services were common before 1914.[2]

The continued existence of ageing steam-hauled suburban rolling stock was a matter of continual public and press criticism. But not many serious and informed writers in the 1930s went so far as to argue that the railways' policy was misguided and that the economics of electrification were so favourable that shortage of investment funds was no real excuse for continued reliance upon steam, although one railway officer interviewed agreed that it might have been false economy to shrink from electrification, since the maintenance cost of the elderly steam stock was rising. 'To keep them up to date and refurbish them regularly was a tremendous item of cost which had to be looked at very carefully.'[3]

Public and press criticisms were eventually much reduced by the announcements of government assistance for railway electrification under the New Works programmes, 1935–40, which included the Shenfield suburban electrification on the LNER, and various London Transport Underground extensions designed to reduce the overcrowding and pressure on both the Great Eastern and the Great Northern suburban lines. It seems to have been accepted that these projects, conceived primarily as a means of reducing unemployment and stimulating the economy in accordance with the new Keynesian doctrine of 'pump priming', did not require precise financial justification. In modern phraseology, their favourable social cost-benefit rate of return was taken for granted.

It is interesting to recall that the Weir Committee on Main Line Electrification included among its members Sir Ralph Wedgwood. The committee was much concerned with the creation of a national electric power network – the 'Grid' – through the new Central Electricity Board, and a heavy railway traction demand from the Grid would probably have improved the justification for capital expenditure upon a high-tension distribution network. The railways, of course, still to a substantial extent generated their own traction current, the Southern at Durnsford Road and Deptford, the LMS at Stonebridge Park, for example. That, however, applied essentially to suburban rail networks; the economics of main-line electrification depended largely upon the price of current to be drawn from the Grid, which in turn depended very much upon load factor.

Wedgwood was also a member of the Central Electricity Board, but his attitude to railway electrification, enthusiastic in 1931, had changed by 1938.[4] Hannah is not surprised by this coolness; he points out, however, that 'railway electrification went as far in Britain as in other countries which lacked cheap hydraulic power'.[5] This point is, of course, essential; comparison between the percentage of track electrified in Britain and in, say, Switzerland, Sweden, or Norway prior to 1939 turns essentially upon the price and availability of bulk supplies of hydro-electric power.

Actually, the group companies, apart from the Southern, seemed cooler in their attitude towards main-line electrification than some of their constituent companies had been. Before the war, and perhaps in a more favourable economic climate, decisions in principle had been taken by the Board of the North Eastern Railway to electrify between York and Newcastle, and by the Board of the London Brighton & South Coast Railway to electrify from London to Brighton. The latter scheme had to wait until it was executed by the Southern on a different system to that proposed by the LBSCR in 1935, whilst the LNER permanently shelved the York–Newcastle project. This may have been a mistake; but it must be remembered that the electrification schemes carried out by the London & North Western, the North Eastern, the Lancashire & Yorkshire – and above all the London & South Western and the London Brighton & South Coast – were all of a suburban nature; no one in Britain had yet ventured into the field of main-line electification.

One retired railwayman defended the policy of the companies in these terms. 'I think it is worth recalling the attitude of all the British railway companies to electrification in those days. The Southern had electrified its suburban system. It was regarded in those days as being a perfectly sound and sensible thing to electrify your suburban operations if they were large enough to warrant it. A great effort was made by the Southern and obviously paid off.

'On the other hand, the other railways, particularly the LMS and Great Western, had not got suburban operations on anything like the scale of the Southern and the real question for them was, was it worth while going in for long-distance electrification? My own personal view is that it would have been extremely difficult for them to have undertaken the capital effort of main-line electrification. It would have been an enormous task, and there would have been a lot of displaced assets and equipment which had not ended its useful life and would have had to have been thrown away.'[6] This view obviously discounts the experience of the Southern, that electrification almost always generates additional traffic in excess of expectations – the so-called 'sparks effect'.

From time to time critics pointed to the expansion of electric traction on the Continent, but in general the stock railway answers – Britain's ample supplies of excellent locomotive coal, eminence in steam locomotive design, and freedom from lengthy mountain sections of line, as for example in Switzerland – went unchallenged. It was the Weir Report that introduced a controversial note, and the proponents of electric traction deplored the railways' inaction following the Weir Committee's broadly favourable view of the overall economic case for electrification. However, the committee appended to its report two case studies prepared by eminent consulting electrical engineers, Messrs Merz & McLellan. The first of these pilot projects covered the LNER lines from King's Cross to Doncaster and Leeds, together with some branches in Lincolnshire. The net capital outlay was estimated at £8,646,000 and the return on this was put at 7·22 per cent, entirely derived from savings in working costs.

The second scheme was for electrification of the LMS main line from Crewe to Carlisle, and Weaver Junction to Liverpool, together with certain branches. The net capital outlay was put at £5,123,370 (a good example of spurious accuracy in estimating!) and the return on this outlay, again derived entirely from savings in working expenses, was no more than 2·5 per cent.

Neither of these schemes was proceeded with. The LNER was short of resources for investment, and the return on the LMS scheme was clearly unattractive.

The Great Western twice considered electrification, to the extent of commissioning reports from consultants. The first related to the handling of coal traffic in the South Wales valleys; the estimated return proved to be uneconomic. The second and much more important study covered the main line from Taunton to Penzance, including branches, and was commissioned in February 1938 from Merz & McLellan.

In the spring of 1939 the GWR announced that it had been decided not to proceed with this scheme. The net capital outlay was around £4 million and the return (again derived entirely from savings in operating expenses) was less than one per cent. This poor return was attributed largely to the high cost of electric locomotives which, surprisingly, would replace steam locomotives on little better than a one-for-one basis. The unbalanced character of the summer peak passenger traffic over this route was also stated to be a main cause of the unfavourable economics. (One may wonder therefore why this route was studied in preference to, say, the London–Bristol–South Wales line.) The decision to go no further may not have been entirely unwelcome to some of the more conservative elements in management both at Paddington and Swindon.

The calculated results from the two schemes appended to the Weir Report were not intended to cast doubt on the main conclusions, which were favourable to electrification. The committee was of opinion that a virtually complete electrification of the country's main-line railways would attract a return of 7 per cent, based upon substantial savings in operating and maintenance charges, which was more than adequate to cover the cost of borrowing the funds required. These estimates ignored the possibility of increased traffic receipts, despite the encouraging experiences of the Southern Railway with suburban electrification.

Bagwell comments that 'the report could not have appeared at a worse time. The national budget was unbalanced and the Treasury and the May Committee were demanding rigid economy in government expenditure. In any case many leading railwaymen were more interested in improving the performance of the steam locomotive than in making exhaustive enquiry into the economics of electric traction. Consequently a very promising scheme was still-born. It was one of the great missed opportunities of the 1930s.'[7]

Regret for the 'missed opportunity' was expressed by the Lord President of the Council, Herbert (Lord) Morrison, in the debate on the second reading of the Transport Bill, 1946, recalling his position as Minister of Transport in 1931. 'The railways said 7 per cent was not enough . . . I think they were wrong, because I think that the cleaner and brighter railways it would have brought would have paid them. They also said they wanted to know how much, if any, subsidy the State would give to enable them to do it. I pointed out to the railway companies that if they had got to the position in which they would not give a decision on electrification until they knew whether or not the State would subsidize it, "You have degenerated into a poor-law frame of mind that will utterly undermine capital and the private enterprise industry in the railways if you go on." But that is where they had got to. It was a confession that they could not adequately do the job.'[8]

The Railway Companies' Association reacted angrily to the charge. 'This is a complete misrepresentation of the facts. What actually occurred regarding the alleged "7 per cent return" was as follows:

'Having made an examination of the economics of electrifying portions of the L.M.S. and L.N.E.R. systems, the Weir Committee considered that to secure full economic advantage it would be necessary to electrify practically the entire Main Line railway system of the country which could be done in from 15 to 20 years, involving capital expenditure by the railways to the extent of £261,000,000, on which the return would be about 7 per cent, and £80,000,000 by the Central Electricity Board.

'The Committee pointed out that there were many factors which might affect the accuracy of their estimates of expenditure and income – in fact, as their report states, "Put shortly, the risks involved in undertaking a comprehensive programme cannot be predicted with accuracy. They lie in the fallability of estimates, in the possibilities of reduction in traffic due to further development of road transport, or to reduced national activity, and finally, in the field of speculative scientific development."

'The report was considered by the railways, and the Chairman of the Railway Companies' Association informed the Minister that while general electrification would be of material assistance in bringing about the general electrical development of the country, and might enable substantial savings in railway working expenses to be realized, the results reached by the Committee were open to a wide margin of error, and important changes in traffics and wages, which would adversely affect the result, had already taken place.

'In view of the speculative nature of the proposal, its magnitude and general conditions, the raising of the capital sum involved would be impracticable, but the Companies were prepared to go forward with definite schemes.

'In the same year (1931), a general financial crisis occurred and all traffics fell heavily.'[9]

The final sentence perhaps identifies the principal reason why no progress was made on the Weir Committee's proposals. The mental attitude created by the depression was unfavourable to enterprise – at least in the early part of the slump – and reluctance or inability to invest was wholly understandable to contemporaries until the 'public works' theory first put forward by Joseph Chamberlain in 1885, and restated by Keynes, began to lead to some special government assistance for railway investments, including the first main-line electrification scheme, that from Manchester to Sheffield and Wath.

An LMS view supported the suggestion that in 1931 government financial aid would have been needed for main-line electrification. 'They looked at the whole of the cost of introducing main-line electrification into the London Midland, based on Weir's elements. They came to the conclusion that the advantage compared to the present was so small that without the assurance of some competitive basis, which they had not got, they dare not take that step in the shareholders' interests and this they told the shareholders in plain terms. If you had been Chairman of, say, the London Midland or the Great Western – the Great Western is a different story, but never mind – the London Midland, you have got shareholders and you are paying 4 per cent on your Ordinary and if you had spent this money, which they could have done, without an assurance and knowing that the cost was so small of advantage to them, the probability is that they would have gone down the drain.'[10]

Lord Stamp had defended this attitude in his statement at the LMS annual general meeting on 12 March 1933 in these words: 'Close consideration has recently been given to further suburban electrification and the general question of main-line electrification. Although our inquiries are not complete, there does not appear to be any likelihood of any further large-scale outlay in the immediate future. We have a statutory obligation to show annually to the Railway Rates Tribunal that our affairs have been conducted with efficiency and economy, quite apart from the Board's obligation to you in this respect, and any new outlay for electrification or anything else must comply with that test. If any new work is unlikely in due course to pay its way, clearly the burden will fall on railway users generally, or the proprietors or employees, or partly one or another. Such outlay differs from the competitive expenditure on public roads for motor traction, which causes a charge on rates, whether the expenditure is commercially justified or not.

'Those who talk glibly on the subject without knowledge of the facts may not bother much about this aspect, but we have to do so. The merits and amenities of electricity have to be weighed against the merits of other forms of tractive power, with due regard to the risk involved in new outlay on fixed plant in the present still indefinite position of the finance of the public roads.'

Whether glibly or not, later writers have attacked the failure to move into electric traction in the 1930s. Aldcroft, for instance, writes that 'the move by British Railways into diesel and electric traction in the 1960s provides an interesting case study of delayed response in the application of new techniques. . . . Given the advantages of diesel and electric traction it is difficult, at least from the standpoint of the 1960s, to see why they were neglected so long. . . . Most of the technical problems had been solved by the 1930s, and many of the benefits, especially of electrification, were apparent well before 1939.'[11]

In similar vein Dyos and Aldcroft comment that 'in view of the advantages of electrification it is surprising that the policy was not more widely adopted'.[12] Aldcroft looks for an historical or semi-psychological reason. 'The railways continued to maintain their faith in steam. Generations of railwaymen – directors, engineers, traffic managers and workmen alike – had been reared in the era of steam traction, and they were reluctant to depart from established practice. . . . Reaction to the new techniques tended, therefore, to be defensive in the sense that serious attempts were made, especially in the 1930s, to improve the performance of the locomotive and speed up existing steam services.'[13]

If such a managerial attitude existed it might be presumed to have been strongest on the Great Western, the only group company that had no electric traction at all. But a vigorous rebuttal came from that quarter. 'I do not think it is a fair criticism at all. As I have already said, it was, I think rightly, decided that there was not much scope for suburban electrification. A very detailed study was made of electrification west of Exeter, and, to my mind, this was probably looking in the right direction for the kind of hauls on which you would get a maximum economic benefit from electrification: heavy loads up steep gradients. The plan did not go forward, for reasons that we discussed earlier – the difficulties of raising the capital. Subsequent developments in electification tariffs and the high cost of peak demand for current make electrification of stopping trains which use a lot of current in stopping and starting an expensive business. The Great Western was not against electrification, but I think, in view of the particular traffics for which it had to cater, looked in a different direction and showed a degree of foresight.'[14]

A postscript to this was quite pungent. 'The real steam lobby developed after the Railway Executive was set up [in 1948] and was on the whole an LMS lobby.'[15]

It is, however, interesting that one LNER view agreed that there was a lukewarm attitude to electrification on that railway. 'It came reluctantly with the decision to electrify to Shenfield. . . . I think they said, "Look, we shall have to show willing about the Weir Report and the government assistance, so we'll do two experimental schemes: Manchester–Sheffield freight electrification, and the Shenfield." There was no wholehearted Herbert Walker push behind this.'[16]

Apart from the scale of electrification, there is a question whether the right system was adopted, particularly on the Southern. In view of certain problems with the third-rail system – the difficulties in track maintenance, icing-up in winter, displaced collector shoes, for instance –

the decision to abandon the Brighton section's overhead a.c. system and replace it with the London & South Western's choice of third-rail d.c. might have been criticised. But in fact the Southern's policy went largely unchallenged. One factor was undoubtedly the inability to use alternating current at the industrial frequency of 50 Hz at that time. The LBSC system of 6,600 V a.c., single-phase, 25 Hz, was of course less efficient than modern high-voltage a.c. systems. This was recalled by one former Southern Railway officer very clearly. 'I knew the Brighton electrification; I was a young man at the time. Working on the line was not such a wonderful thing, I mean those motor vans were very heavy. The acceleration was very poor and the voltage would have been a mystery these days. Do not overlook the very many tight clearances that existed on the SECR. Raworth – a progressive engineer – had designed for the SECR a system, which while different from the one adopted on the LSWR, was nevertheless a conductor rail concept.'[17] In short, the point was made that the Walker choice of third-rail 'was the right decision at the time and certainly the decision was right for a quarter of a century'.[18]

The Southern's electrification programme was well under way when the Pringle Committee on systems of railway electrification reported in 1928. The voltage recommended for future use was 1,500 V d.c. with overhead transmission, the d.c. 750 V third-rail system also being approved and, possibly in future, 3,000 V d.c. with overhead transmission. (It was noteworthy that the Electrical Engineer of the Southern Railway, and a member of the committee, declined to support these recommendations.) Incidentally, the Pringle Committee's preferred system, 1,500 V d.c., was incorporated in the Weir Committee studies and it was of course used for the LNER electrification projects in the 1935–40 New Works programme.

In the field of diesel traction there is a fairly sharp difference between contemporary writers, who saw little wrong with the limited, even hesitant moves towards the new form of traction, and later critics such as Aldcroft, who suggests that 'in America diesel traction gained ground rapidly from the middle of the 1930s. By 1940 diesel power was responsible for one eighth of the ton mileage, one-quarter of the passenger car mileage, and one-third of the shunting and marshalling mileage on American railroads, and the American companies had practically abandoned the construction of new steam locomotives.'[19]

On this point the US railroads' move into diesel traction in the 1930s had concentrated upon lightweight high-speed streamlined units, and the massive change-over to diesel power for freight came later. A typically progressive US line, the Atchison Topeka & Santa Fé, which had introduced the diesel 'Super-Chief' streamliner in 1936 between Chicago and Los Angeles, in 1946 had 1,567 steam locomotives in service, only 374 diesel units for line-haul work, usually in multiple, and 144 diesel switching locomotives.[20]

It is of course easy to point out that the dieselisation of American railroads was largely promoted and financed by a powerful motor industry, and particularly by General Motors, to which there was no counterpart in Britain; that diesel fuel was relatively cheap in the USA and that other factors were present such as the high cost of locomotive water supplies on certain sections of line. Britain on the other hand enjoyed ample supplies of large coal suitable for locomotives and universal water supplies. Lastly, of course, when war came it was a great relief that the railways depended almost entirely upon home-produced fuel and made virtually no demands on oil imported at a heavy cost in ships and lives.

The ventures into diesel traction were of two kinds – light 'railcar' units for use on branch and secondary lines, and shunting locomotives. In the first field the Great Western was pre-eminent with its fleet of AEC-built railcars, which by 1939 had been increased to eighteen units; and in the second, the LMS was well satisfied with its stock of thirty-eight diesel-electric and diesel-mechanical shunters in the same year. The LNER and the Southern had made only a token investment in these forms of traction.

In addition, there had been some isolated experiments with the internal combustion engine which led nowhere – the LMS 'Ro-railer', the LNER 'Tyneside Venturer' railcar and the LMS three-car diesel set that ran for a time on a cross-country service between Oxford and Cambridge via Bletchley. None of these had any lasting significance; it was only in the post-war period, really outside the scope of this study, that the first experimental main-line diesel locomotives were ordered – two each on the Southern and the LMS, whilst the GWR went so far as to order two gas turbine locomotives and the LNER Board approved in principle a scheme for diesel traction on the East Coast main line. It is a matter of history that these developments were not followed up after nationalisation, until the Modernisation Plan for British Railways was launched in 1955.

Turning from traction policy to the handling of freight, there is a long history of criticism by outside observers, sometimes well informed and sometimes less so. The main target has been the railways' adherence to the low-capacity four-wheeled wagon, loose-coupled and devoid of a power brake. As early as 1902 Sir George Paish[21] was making in *The Statist* a long series of statistical comparisons of the performance of British railways with those of the USA, to the disadvantage of the former. Incidentally, in an introduction to the book reproducing the *Statist* articles, George Stegmann Gibb,[22] then General Manager of the North Eastern Railway, agreed that 'more can be done than has been done in the direction of increasing train loads and waggon [*sic*] loads in England'.[23]

Many subsequent critics followed the Paish arguments, well into the 1930s. Not many General Managers were quite as broad-minded as Gibb; the NER of course had managed to handle its vast coal traffic with larger wagons – often of 20 tons capacity – than most other railways, and it was an ardent propagandist for statistical measurements of operating efficiency.

But by 1928 W. V. (Sir William) Wood, then Controller of Costs and Statistics of the LMS, was writing that 'the outstanding characteristic of the British stock compared with that of other countries is its small unit capacity and the variety of its ownership. In its origin the British railway was regarded merely as a special type of highway, over which anyone could run his locomotive or vehicles on payment of a toll, but at an early stage the locomotives and carriages were solely railway-owned and only the wagons were provided by users, and then only for certain traffics, mainly coal and other minerals. There are now 721,000 wagons owned by the railway companies for public traffic and about 600,000 wagons owned by traders, and, of the latter, about 550,000 are used for coal traffic.

'As the coal wagons require to be sorted into ownership order and returned to their owners, usually empty, the restricted use of them is a handicap to the railways; but the system has continued for 100 years and is claimed by many to be justified by the nature of the British coal trade. All over the country there are retail dealers in small quantities of coal, who prefer buying a few wagonloads in hired wagons, and leisurely loading their road-delivery vehicles from the wagons as customers' orders are received.'[24]

Wood advocated the pooling of both railway and private owners' wagons and the use of larger wagons for coal. He wrote: 'If 20-ton wagons were standard and were loaded to only 17½ tons on the average, a considerable saving would be effected . . . the superiority of the larger wagon is marked. The length of the train and consequent siding necessity is reduced by 11 per cent; the weight to be hauled, apart from the brake van, is reduced by 11 per cent; the actual tractive effort for a given gross tonnage is less . . . the cost and therefore interest on capital is 17 per cent less and the maintenance of wagons is reduced. There is also a reduction of 40 per cent in the number of wagons with consequential reductions, though not in so great a ratio, in the cost of shunting.'[25]

It cannot therefore be said that the railways were entirely complacent about their use of small wagons, but, under private ownership of coal mining and distribution, the chances of reform were not put very high by Wood. 'A change over to larger wagons would not be possible in all cases without, probably, a large outlay on alterations of the screens or other equipment at the collieries, the tipping appliances at ports, and the turntables, traversers and loading arrangements in railway yards. The further difficulty already referred to in connexion with the customers of the retail coal trade has also to be considered, but the balance is greatly in favour of universal use of, and larger capacity of, coal-wagon stock.'[26]

Wood considered the chance of using larger wagons for merchandise as opposed to mineral traffic to be even smaller. In 1926 on the LMS the average weight per consignment had been between 5 and 6 cwt. He added: 'With the small size of consignments in Great Britain, there does not appear to be any probability of any marked increase in the merchandise wagon capacity, not does that appear to be desirable, except, perhaps, for the few trades which forward large consignments to one station. A hopeful sign is the growing system of forwarding full wagon loads to central depots from which the consignor then distributes the quantities required by his customers.'[27]

There was a steady if not spectacular growth in the number of merchandise (not mineral) wagons fitted with the vacuum brake and screw couplings which could run at higher speeds where this was called for in the case of regular traffic flows between important centres. These 'fitted freights' usually provided an overnight service. Most of them ran to a strict timetable and some carried names which, usually starting as nicknames bestowed by the staff, later became officially adopted as possessing sales appeal.

Where 'fully fitted' trains could not be made up, partially braked trains were sometimes marshalled to include wagons that were piped for continuous braking although without such brakes themselves, or trains containing unbraked wagons ran with a 'fitted head' comprising a number of vacuum-braked wagons marshalled next to the engine and thus providing extra braking power. Such trains were permitted to run at higher speeds than the ordinary unbraked goods train.

It must be remembered that although the four group companies had all decided to standardise the vacuum brake, they had inherited from some former constituents and subsidiaries a substantial number of locomotives and carriage equipped with the Westinghouse air brake, and the change-over process was slow and costly.

The reasons why the small wagon continued to be unequipped, for the most part, with continuous brakes and screw couplings were mainly the costs, both capital and capital maintenance, of a change-over applied to the huge total stock of over 1,300,000 wagons. So Wood's argument does have some relevance to Aldcroft's sweeping criticism that 'Freight handling methods remained grossly inefficient. Bulk consignments of freight moving at high speed in through trains were the exception rather than the rule. Railway wagons were too small, too lightly loaded and badly marshalled.'[28]

It is of course arguable that the railways could have struggled more effectively against the handicaps to which Wood referred. Something certainly was achieved. The north-east had a regional practice under which the railway normally provided the wagons for the coal shipment trade, and these were usually 20 ton hoppers. Effective operation and relatively good turn-rounds were achieved. The Great Western offered a rebate for coal shipped in 20 ton wagons, with some degree of success. The Midland Railway had much earlier embarked upon an ambitious scheme of buying up private-owner wagons, which failed to achieve its object, as the compensation money was simply applied to the purchase of new wagons!

Outside observers continued to be struck by the cost and delay which the traditional system of freight handling – pick-up stopping trains, often lightly loaded, sorting and marshalling in sidings and yards with intermediate 'trip' workings – involved. Their criticisms may be considered to have been substantiated by the transformation which took place in the 1960s and 1970s when British Railways changed to a concentration upon trainload operations and the Freightliner road–rail network. But this followed a massive transfer to road transport of the 'retail' type of consignment to which Wood had alluded as being at the root of the traditional railway handling methods. The Freightliner system had been foreshadowed to some extent as early as 1912 by A. W. Gattie,[29] who formed his New Transport Company to promote his scheme for universal 'containerisation' of freight train traffic with road–rail interchange at huge mechanised transfer depots, only one of which he envisaged as being required for London. Gattie was in many ways right in his vision of a better apportionment of functions as between road and rail, and the need to mechanise and speed up inter-modal transfers. He came into conflict with conventional railway policy, and his rather abrasive personality and his eagerness to enter into controversy seem to have hindered rather than helped acceptance of his ideas, which were described in a book rather fancifully entitled *How to Make the Railways Pay for the War.*[30]

An illustration of the railway management reaction is the instruction received by a young officer to take the Gattie scheme and pull it to pieces in a report for his superiors.[31]

Towards the end of the period under study the railways often claimed that, within a framework set more by the pattern of British industry and trade than by railway operating policies, they were making steady progress in improving their efficiency in freight handling. At the LMS annual general meeting in March 1940 Lord Stamp announced that in 1939 train miles per engine hour had increased by over 7 per cent compared with 1929 and wagon miles per engine hour by over 9 per cent.

An LNER view, already quoted, was that 'by the mid-1930s . . . the whole of the freight service had been shaken up and reorganised'[32] in East Anglia and in the north-east. The improvement in speed of the general merchandise traffic, as opposed to coal and minerals, where time savings are not so important, was described as a *tour de force*. A bold claim was made that 'by 1939 when the war came there was no question that the railways were probably at their peak of efficiency, that is, for carrying goods and people; they were probably better than they had ever been since amalgamation in 1923'.[33]

The railways had, of course, as described in Chapter 4, been moving steadily if not very rapidly towards promoting the use of containers, albeit not yet on the later Freightliner principle and still less on the universal basis advocated by Gattie.

Turning from operating practice to research, historians have not levelled much criticism at the railways for omitting to undertake fundamental research and, for the most part, confining themselves to routine testing of materials. Individual Chief Mechanical Engineers built experimental locomotives such as Gresley's and Fowler's high-pressure locomotives and Stanier's isolated turbine engine. More fundamental research was really confined to the LMS, which supported a substantial research department at Derby under the direct control of a Vice-President, Sir Harold Hartley. One of his former assistants considered that 'he did very well in the research sphere. Whether all research was good, bad or indifferent I do not know, but he singled out that particular function for a bit of a boost which it had not had in any other of the main-line companies. There had not been a separate research organisation, it had all been done through the engineering departments.

'The scale was very small compared with what BR are doing now. But it started with quite a good man in charge of it, Herbert. Herbert was in his time particularly active. He formalised the research function in the LMS Railway Company and I think that was a forerunner of the kind of research activity that has gone on in the railways since and which has reached its climax in the research centre at Derby, which has made its name world-wide.'[34]

A point of some importance was the relationship between the engineers and the scientists, which since nationalisation has sometimes been difficult. Co-operation did exist on the LMS. 'For example, Stanier[35] was brought in as the Chief Mechanical Engineer. He was constantly in session with Sir Harold Hartley; so were the other engineers. They were all good in their fields and their work. They were not just career railwaymen who had gone to seed.'[36]

The example of the LMS was not followed by the other railways,[37] though main workshops such as those at Doncaster and Swindon certainly had laboratories mainly employed in materials testing and analysis. Outside assistance was from time to time involved, as when Gresley utilised the wind tunnel at Imperial College, London, for his experiments with streamlining the A4 Pacific locomotives.

If there was little public criticism of the railways in this rather specialised field, there may well have been some dissatisfaction among civil servants at the Ministry of Transport. Otherwise it is difficult to see the reason for Section 4(3) of the Transport Act, 1947, which required that 'in the exercise and performance of their functions as to . . . research, the Commission shall act on lines settled as aforesaid' – i.e. with the approval of the Minister.

To sum up the attitude of the railway managements to technical change and innovation in a phrase is quite impossible. In some respects they were forward-looking, in others perhaps too conservative. Examples of modest but useful improvements in, especially, permanent way and signalling have been quoted in Chapter 5. However, dominating their policies throughout the whole period was their rather difficult financial position and their sense of obligation to their shareholders. Even so, Bank rate had fallen to 2 per cent in June 1932, and with such cheap money available one may wonder whether it was right to shelve major improvement schemes to protect the short-term position.

Notes

1 A. R. Dunbar (LNER).
2 See T. C. Barker and R. M. Robbins, *A History of London Transport*, vol. II, 1974, pp. 47–8. Also G. F. A. Wilmot, *The Railway in Finchley*, 1962, pp. 25–32.
3 A. R. Dunbar (LNER).
4 See L. Hannah, *Electricity before Nationalisation*, 1979, pp. 161 *seq.*
5 *Ibid.*, p. 166.
6 P. E. Garbutt (LMS).
7 P. S. Bagwell, *The Transport Revolution from 1770*, 1974, p. 257.
8 Hansard, 28 December 1946, col. 2079.
9 Railway Companies' Association, *Criticisms of the Railway arising in Parliamentary Debates and in Press and Public Discussion since the Presentation of the Transport Bill, and the Replies*, 1947, Section 4, *Criticisms regarding the Operational Efficiency of the Railways.*
10 A. J. Pearson (LMS).
11 D. H. Aldcroft, *Studies in British Transport History, 1870–1970*, 1974, p. 243.
12 H. J. Dyos and D. H. Aldcroft, *British Transport*, 1969, p. 332.
13 Aldcroft, *Studies in British Transport History*, p. 254.
14 A. W. Tait (GWR).
15 *Ibid.*
16 G. F. Fiennes (LNER).
17 J. L. Harrington (SR).
18 *Ibid.*
19 *Studies in British Transport History*, p. 243.
20 On the timing of the steam-to-diesel change-over, see John P. Stamer, *Life and Decline of the American Railroad*, 1970, pp. 204–53.
21 Sir George Paish, 1867–1957. Editor of *The Statist* 1900–16, author, economist and adviser to governments.

22 Sir George Stegmann Gibb, 1850–1925. Solicitor, NER, 1882. General Manager, NER, 1891–1906. Director, NER, 1906–10. Chairman, Metropolitan District Railway and London Electric Railways group, 1906–10. Chairman, Roads Board, 1910–19.

23 G. Paish, *The British Railway Position*, 1902.

24 W. V. Wood and Sir Josiah Stamp, *Railways*, p. 82.

25 *Ibid.*, p. 85.

26 *Ibid.*, p. 87.

27 *Ibid.*, p. 87.

28 D. H. Aldcroft, *British Transport since 1914*, p. 40.

29 A. W. Gattie, 1856–1925. Inventor, author and journalist. Chairman, New Transport Company.

30 R. Horniman, *How to Make the Railways Pay for the War*, 1916.

31 Private information from the late D. R. Lamb.

32 G. F. Fiennes (LNER).

33 A. J. Pearson (LMS).

34 P. E. Garbutt (LMS).

35 Sir William A. Stanier, FRS, 1876–1956. Works Manager, Swindon, GWR, 1920–22. Principal Assistant to Chief Mechanical Engineer, GWR, 1922–31. Chief Mechanical Engineer, LMS, 1932–44. Principal Scientific Adviser, Ministry of Production, 1942–48.

36 P. E. Garbutt (LMS).

37 Except perhaps in the joint LMS/LNER scheme for a joint locomotive testing station at Rugby, started before the war but only completed after it.

9

A summing-up: the managers' reply to the historians' verdict

It emerges faily clearly from the previous chapters that the judgements of historians about railway policy have often been over-simplified. One reason is that the four grouped companies did not always act in unison, despite the existence of the co-ordinating machinery of the Railway Clearing House and the Railway Companies' Association. Another is that, although policies might be agreed and appear clear-cut, their application might vary considerably. There is thus a danger in either criticising or endorsing 'railway policy' in general terms.

Equally, when one turns from policy to achievement, it is clear that the quality of the service provided to the travelling public and to the consignors of goods varied between the excellent and the pretty unsatisfactory. Neither the self-congratulatory publicity issued by, for instance, the LMS, nor on the other hand Aldcroft's sweeping statement that 'freight handling methods remained grossly inefficient', can be relied upon to give a fair picture of a complex situation.

But it is interesting that there is no straightforward distinction between some historians sharply criticising what was done, and former managers consistently defending it. Several historians try to balance achievements against shortcomings; managers often admit that, even if cardinal errors were avoided, the services were not all that they should have been.

Company origins often coloured the managers' remarks. It is noticeable that those with a Great Western or Southern background were the most inclined to view the past with satisfaction. The Great

Western certainly promoted a very strong family spirit and loyalty which in turn were unlikely to see much wrong with the policies that the company pursued. The Southern attitude was basically that the inter-war years had been a time of efficient and aggressive management, pursuing a realistic policy of improving services as rapidly as external circumstances, especially financial resources, would permit. Relatively little specific criticism was directed at the Southern, and in consequence there was little need to adopt a strongly defensive posture.

If the Great Western was inclined to refute any charge of complacency by arguing that the established methods by which it carried on its business suited its customers and the territory it served, the Southern was changing so fast that it saw little to refute. The team headed by Sir Herbert Walker enjoyed an exhilarating participation in a programme that, if not aiming at the ideal, would nevertheless markedly improve the quality of service.

Rather different attitudes are to be found coming from the LNER and the LMS. The LNER spokesmen showed a considerable respect and even affection for their old company but were fairly outspoken about its shortcomings and difficulties, many simply due to the fact that it served not merely the dryer side of Britain – as it advertised – but also much of the poorer side. To some extent this outspokenness may have had its origins in the tradition, tolerated by Robert Bell and others, of pretty frank discussion of company policy even by comparatively junior officers – something that was not encouraged on the more authoritarian LMS. At a higher level it was reflected in the debates between the three Areas of the LNER, whose Divisional General Managers seldom saw quite eye-to-eye.

The LMS, as the largest company and the one whose problems were correspondingly great, was defended strongly by several spokesmen, but was not immune from criticism, particularly by one who had left the company comparatively early in his career. Where the historians have criticised 'the railways' it is most often the LMS which comes to mind as the archetype. It seems to emerge that the LMS achieved much in the inter-war years yet retained some shortcomings that were not so simply attributable to a serious shortage of financial resources as were the corresponding deficiencies on the LNER.

An interesting feature of the differing views of historians and managers is the way in which a sudden and illuminating comment by one of the latter can turn upside down some generally accepted thesis repeated by more than one historian. Take for instance Feinstein's argument, repeated by Aldcroft and others as a criticism of the railway managements, that there was net 'disinvestment' in the infrastructure between 1923 and 1939. It produced the vigorous rejoinder that *of course* this was the case: it had in fact been one of the objectives of the amalgamation Act of 1921. Had there been no reduction in the scale of the assets employed in the business the Boards would have been in dereliction of their duty.

Another example is the repeated criticism that the railways were very ignorant about costs, and that they should have related their charges to them much more closely. Nothing could be more trenchant than the comment that 'the railways have lost a very large quantity of traffic through fussing about costs and trying to calculate direct costs. With a railway . . . it pays, on the whole, to maximise the use of the tracks and the rolling stock in terms of locomotion and vehicles, and you cannot improve on the Acworth dictum of charging what the traffic will bear and getting as much traffic as you can within sensible limits.'[1]

It would be wrong to consider the managers' comments as mainly nostalgic, though there was a general view that management could often act more effectively forty years ago, to which the union representative did not dissent. The constraints were fewer and the freedom of action greater. On the other hand the system, particularly at middle management levels, was not without its petty bureaucrats. The departmental system of organisation probably fostered this. But there was very little criticism of the men at the top – figures such as Stamp, Milne, Wedgwood and Walker – though their impact upon the railway – as Chapters 1 and 2 have shown – varied a good deal.

One danger besetting historians, highlighted several times, is that of criticising a failure to employ techniques that scarcely existed, if at all, in the 1920s and 1930s. Examples can be found in traffic costing and staff productivity. Perhaps one may argue that the science (or art) of traffic costing did not have to wait upon any scientific or technological breakthrough and so it could have been developed much earlier. The fact is that nowhere in the world was it effectively practised – and this despite the efforts of the Interstate Commerce Commission in the USA.

As for labour productivity, the seeds of work study certainly existed but were scarcely flowering in industry generally. Not until the 1950s could they be transplanted into certain limited fields of railway civil engineering practice. The basic technology for increasing the productivity of traffic staff – especially diesel traction and signalling concentration schemes based upon advanced electronics – was only partially available before the war.

The field of commercial policy and charges is that to which the economic historians have directed most of their criticisms of railway policy. But the two major points, as already remarked, are mutually inconsistent.

The first runs like this. The railways should not have carried so much of their low-rated heavy traffics – coal, iron ore, etc. – at 'exceptional' rates below standard. On the contrary, since they enjoyed a virtual monopoly in this range of traffic, they should have pushed up the rates. The additional profits from this source would have enabled them to reduce the rates on the traffics for which they were in competition with the road hauliers, namely the higher-rated 'general merchandise' classes.

The second argument is that the railways should have related their charges much more closely to costs, attracting new business where their costs were low and letting the traffic go elsewhere where their costs were so high as to make a cost-based rate uncompetitive.

The flaw in these criticisms is that the relationship between cost and price varied considerably – but it was a variation that showed the low-rated commodities to be the most profitable, as was rapidly established when a Traffic Costing Service was created after nationalisation. The main difference turned on the load factor. In 1938, for instance, the average wagonload of 'minerals and heavy merchandise' was 9·8 tons. The average receipts per ton mile were 0·96*d* (0·4p), yielding average earnings per wagon mile of 9·4*d* (3·9p). The corresponding figures for coal showed earnings of 10·5*d* (4·4p) per wagon mile.

But the higher-rated traffics, which some commentators suggested should have been charged less, produced an average wagonload in the same year of 2·8 tons and average receipts per ton mile were only 2·0*d* (0·8p), yielding an average receipt per wagon mile of only 5·6*d* (2p). And the 'general merchandise' traffic handling costs were increased by the considerable terminal expenses, whereas most of the heavy traffics were to and from 'private sidings' – industrial premises, coal mines, merchants' coal yards, and so on. As an article in *Modern Transport* claimed, 'the railways carry practically all the coal, minerals and heavy merchandise traffic available to them at rates which are profitable to the railways and which represent all that these traffics can bear. The total gross revenue secured thereby, however, is not nearly enough to carry the fixed costs of the railways, and it is therefore essential that the railways shall continue to carry a substantial proportion of the "general merchandise" traffic susceptible to road competition. This traffic is carried at much higher average costs than the heavy traffic, and in consequence yields a lower average margin over the direct cost of moving it, despite higher charges. Nevertheless it enables the overheads to be spread over a sufficiently large volume of gross receipts, and its retention is therefore imperative if the railways are to remain self-supporting.'[2]

This general thesis is not so far removed from the generality of the comments made by the managers in reply to the criticisms of the historians. To put up the rates on the 'backbone' traffics – coal, minerals, steel, etc. – would have increased the costs of industry substantially and would – quite apart from the statutory controls of the Railway Rates Tribunal – have probably induced the government to intervene. On the other hand, reducing the rates on much of the general merchandise would, if the traffic was still being retained to rail, merely have presented a bonus to the traders but would have reduced profit margins that were already inadequate and sometimes non-existent.

Equally, cost-based rates would have presented heavy industry with a bonus but involved the railways in a heavy loss of revenue, since little or no extra traffic could be expected in an area where demand was so inelastic. Conversely, raising the rates on 'general merchandise' would have accelerated the already considerable loss of traffic to the roads and narrowed the overall base of gross receipts which, as *Modern Transport* pointed out, was essential to cover the fixed costs of the infrastructure.

Whether or not the managements were complacent or apathetic in the situation in which they were placed is difficult to judge. There were certainly keen intellects engaged in the business of charging policy, able to defend the course taken very trenchantly. But it also seems clear that many managers were more interested in the quality of service they could provide than in charges which seemed to be so largely outside their power to control. Here the main regrets were directed at shortage of money to carry out improvements which in principle most of them would have liked to introduce.

On the attitude to technology, the historians who have argued that the railways should have moved much faster and further into electric and diesel traction are answered to some extent by the attention drawn to shortage of investment funds. Although some of the managerial views on this might seem rather reactionary, there was a revealing remark to the effect that the real steam lobby only developed after nationalisation.

It is interesting that several historians repeat, with or without acknowledgment, the criticism of the Royal Commission on Transport that the railways' chief answer to road competition was the attempt 'to get on the road' themselves, and that the sums invested in road transport would have been better spent on improving rail services, e.g. by electrification. None of the managers seemed to accept that the railways were at fault here – or for that matter in the parallel case of railway investment in air transport. It was clear that there were differences in company practice, some railway officers on bus company Boards being under instruction to think as bus men, with the object of improving the profits and hence the yield on the railway investment, whilst others were expected to keep the rail-traffic interest foremost in their minds.

The general trend of management opinion was that the railways were right to diversify; it was only prudent to follow the principle 'If you can't beat them, join them'. Equally, the resources available for such ventures were limited and, for the time being at any rate, it seemed that the railways would continue to be the backbone of the nation's transport, so that securing a foothold was more important than advancing boldly in any particular direction. No doubt if the post-war explosion of road transport had been foreseen a different outlook might have prevailed.

The historians have not made many specific criticisms of personnel policy apart from certain suggestions that railway staff were underpaid. The railways argued during the anti-nationalisation campaign that the Ministry of Transport official *Railways (Staff) Return* for 1947 showed that the average weekly earnings of all men (excluding salaried staff) employed on the railways were slightly higher than the average weekly earnings in all the other principal industries. And, of course, security of employment was pretty well ensured.

But autocratic management was admitted here and there, tempered, however – at any rate on the Great Western – by a certain benevolent paternalism. A telling remark came from that company. 'To quote one small aspect, there was what was known as the Directors' Fund, was financed partly by directors' fees which the directors didn't pick up and partly by the fees that would have been paid to directors had they attended the meetings but didn't . . . there was a certain allocation and if they didn't attend that money went in the kitty. I've known dozens and dozens of cases where, perhaps, you had a signalman whose wife had to go to hospital and he'd run up some debts. You'd only got to put that in writing and send it up to Paddington and ten or twenty pounds (which was quite a lot in those days) would come back without any sort of question. It not only did good to the recipient but I think it created an atmosphere of a sort of closeness with the staff.'[3]

Discipline too on the GWR was tempered with a humanity not perhaps always found on the LMS. 'We had a different approach to the staff irregularities, particularly signalmen's irregularities, than, say, the LMS. It was the inborn habit on the Western that if a signalman, let us say, turned the points between a couple of wagons and got it off the road, the Great Western's natural approach was to say, you know, "Who was the signalman? Oh, Bill Jones. I wouldn't have thought he'd be as stupid as that, I'd like to see him." You'd have him in and you'd find out perhaps that he'd been up all night with his wife who was ill or some reason like that, or he'd a child who'd been rushed off to hospital and his mind was temporarily occupied with some personal worry. It was a mental lapse and we would perhaps give him one day's suspension as a nominal punishment or we would say, "We'll give you a verbal warning, don't do it again." Now I gather that on the LMS – and Tommy Royle told me this one day on Cardiff platform – all staff arrangements were centralised at Crewe. You filled up a form and said that signalman so-and-so and so-and-so violated rule No. 123. Crewe then looked at their ready reckoner and said, "What is the punishment for violating rule 123?" And you had a form back to say that this man must have two days' suspension. The background wasn't taken into account.'[4]

These quotations illustrate the danger of generalising about 'the railways' policy'.

The extent to which the comments of the managers have thrown new light upon the opinions of the historians is not easy to summarise. There is no clear confrontation between two sides. One may hope that some of the harsher judgements might be qualified if histories were to be rewritten, since clearly many situations were more complex than outside observation would indicate. History that is written chiefly from statistics and documents may well need modification when those who helped to shape events recall what the pressures upon them were, and what were the arguments that led to decision-making. Wisdom derived from hindsight can often lead to judgements that fail to penetrate the springs of action.

Notes

1 A. A. Harrison (LNER); see Chapter 4, n. 45.
2 'Swings and roundabouts', *Modern Transport*, 9 September 1944.
3 H. H. Phillips (GWR).
4 A. W. Tait (GWR).

Appendix

Short official biographies of those interviewed

LMS

A. J. Pearson, FCIT

Joined CLC as a clerk, 1918. Resigned from the railway to become Assistant Editor, *Modern Transport*, in 1931. Returned to railway service in 1934 as Personal Assistant to the Vice-President (Finance and Services), LMS. Assistant to Vice-President, 1939. Assistant to President, LMS, 1941. Chief Officer (Administration), the Railway Executive, 1948. Chief of General Duties, British Transport Commission, 1954. Assistant General Manager, London Midland Region, 1958. Retired 1968.

P. E. Garbutt, OBE, FCIT, FIL, FRSA

Joined LMS 1934. Entered Secretary's office, Euston, 1935. Joined personal staff of Vice-President (Research), 1937. War service, 1940–47. Joined London Transport, 1947. Personal Assistant to Board Member (Operations and Engineering), 1948. Planning Assistant (Railways), 1952. Superintendent (New Works), Railways, 1959. Deputy Secretary and Works Officer, 1962. Director of Transportation Policy, 1969. Secretary to the Executive, 1974. Chief Secretary, 1976. Retired 1979.

D. S. M. Barrie, OBE, OStJ, FCIT

Joined LMS Press Section, Euston, in 1932, following eight years' experience in journalism. After war service, appointed Assistant Advertising and Publicity Officer, LMS. Public Relations Officer, the Railway Executive, 1948. Chief Public Relations Officer, British Transport Commission, 1956. Assistant Secretary-General, BTC, 1958. Assistant General Manager, North Eastern Region, 1961. Assistant General Manager, Eastern Region, 1966. Chairman and General Manager, Eastern Region, 1968. Retired 1970.

J. R. Pike, FCIT

Joined LNWR 1914. After war service rejoined railway in Chief Goods Manager's Office, Euston. Personal Assistant to Vice-President, LMS, 1931. Assistant District Goods and Passenger Manager, Leicester, 1933. Assistant to Chief Commercial Manager for (1) Railway Rates Tribunal work; then (2) for research; then (3) for rates and charges. On loan to Railway Executive Committee, 1939. Assistant Chief Commercial Manager (Goods), LMS, 1942. Assistant Chief Commercial Manager, 1946. Chief Officer (Goods), the Railway Executive, 1948. Chief Rates and Charges Officer, the Railway Executive, 1950. Chief Commercial Officer, BR Central Staff, BTC, 1955. Retired 1957. Adviser on charges to East African Railways, 1958. Member of Board of Nyasaland Railways, 1962.

P. J. Fisher, FCIT

Joined LMS, 1928. Posts in Operating Department. After war service, District Operating Manager, Rugby, 1946. District Operating Manager, Liverpool (Lime Street), 1947. Divisional Operating Superintendent, Crewe, London Midland Region, 1956. Traffic Co-ordinating Officer, Euston, 1962. Retired 1969.

LNER

A. R. Dunbar, CBE, FCIT

Joined NBR, 1922. LNER Staff Traffic Apprentice, 1924. Operating Department experience, rising to Assistant District Superintendent (Leeds) and District Superintendent (Manchester). During the war Assistant Superintendent, Southern Area (Eastern Section), LNER. Operating Superintendent, Southern Area (Eastern Section), LNER, 1947. Assistant General Manager, North Eastern Region, 1954. Manpower Adviser, British Transport Commission, 1958. Member of British Railways Board, 1963. President of the Chartered Institute of Transport, 1966–67. Retired 1968.

G. F. Fiennes, OBE, OStJ, MA, FCIT

Educated Winchester and Oxford. Entered LNER as graduate Traffic Apprentice, 1928. Assistant Yardmaster, Whitemoor, 1931. Chief Controller, Cambridge, 1935. Chief Freight Trains Clerk, Liverpool Street. Assistant District Superintendent, Edinburgh. Assistant District Superintendent, Cambridge. Trains Assistant to the Superintendent, North Eastern Area, 1942. District Superintendent, Nottingham, 1943. District Superintendent, Stratford, 1944. Assistant Superintendent, Eastern Region, 1948. Chief Operating Superintendent, Eastern Region, 1956. Line Traffic

Manager (Great Northern), 1957. Chief Operating Officer, British Railways Board, 1961. Chairman and General Manager, Western Region, 1963. Chairman and General Manager, Eastern Region, 1967. Retired 1967.

A. A. Harrison, FCIT

Joined LNWR, 1917. Transferred to NER as Traffic Apprentice, 1922. Assistant to District Goods Manager, Leeds, 1926. Road Motor Superintendent (North Eastern Area), LNER, 1933. Cartage Manager (North Eastern Area), 1940. Assistant Goods Manager (acting) (Southern Area), 1943. District Manager, Cambridge, 1944. Assistant Goods Manager (Rates) (Southern Area), 1945. Assistant Goods Manager (Southern Area), 1946. Executive Officer (Road Transport), the Railway Executive, 1948. Chief Co-ordination Officer, BR Central Staff, British Transport Commission, 1954. Chief Charges Officer, BR Central Staff, BTC, 1955. Chief Freight Officer, BR Central Staff, BTC, 1958. Assistant General Manager (Eastern Region) (Traffic Function), 1960. Retired 1962.

M. A. Cameron, MA, FCIT

Educated Fettes and Edinburgh University. Joined LNER as graduate Traffic Apprentice, 1926. Appointed to Road Transport Section of Passenger Manager's Office, Southern Area, 1929. Assistant London District Passenger Manager, 1935. District Passenger Manager, Leeds, 1937. Acting Passenger Manager (Southern Area), 1939. Acting Passenger Manager (Scottish Area), 1943. Assistant Passenger Manager (Southern Area), 1945. Assistant Secretary (Traffic), British Transport Commission, 1948. Principal Traffic Officer, BTC, 1949. Member, Central Transport Consultative Committee, 1950–62. Principal Officer (Administration), British Railways Board, 1963. Seconded as United Nations Adviser to Malayan Government Railways, 1963. Retired 1964.

G. R. Hayes, MBE, FCIT

Joined M&GN, 1922. Transferred to LNER, Superintendent's Department, Liverpool Street, 1936. Works Section of Chief General Manager's Office, 1940. Personal Assistant to Sir Ralph Wedgwood at Railway Executive Committee, 1941. Head of Finance and Statistics Section, Chief General Manager's Office, 1943. Head of Ancillary Services Section, CGMO, 1945. Senior Executive Assistant, Road Transport Executive, 1948. Disposals Officer, Road Haulage Executive, 1954. Training Officer, British Road Services, 1958. Assistant Secretary (Organisation), BRS, 1958. Assistant Secretary, BRS Federation Ltd, 1963. Acting Chief Officer, National Freight Federation, 1971. Retired 1971.

GWR

A. W. Tait, OBE, FCCA, FCIT

Joined GWR, 1927. During war Assistant Secretary of Railway Executive Committee and Railway Companies' Association Accountants' Committees. Assistant to Chief Accountant, GWR, 1944. Member of Milne Committee on Irish Transport, 1948–49. Director of Costings, British Transport Commission, 1950. Assistant General Manager, Eastern Region, 1956. Deputy General Manager (Finance), British Transport Hotels, 1963. Assistant General Manager (Finance), Southern Region, 1965. Executive Director (Finance), British Railways Board, 1969. Director, Policy Review, 1973–74. Retired 1974.

H. H. Phillips, OBE, FCIT, ACIS

Joined GWR, 1908. Personal staff of General Manager until 1932. Office of Superintendent of the Line, 1932. Assistant Divisional Operating Superintendent, Cardiff, 1937. Divisional Operating Superintendent, Cardiff, 1941. Assistant to Superintendent of the Line, 1948. Assistant Chief Regional Officer, Western Region, 1948. Chief Commercial Officer, the Railway Executive, 1950. Chief Commercial Officer, British Transport Commission, 1953. Assistant General Manager, Western Region, 1954. Retired 1957, and appointed a member of the Transport Tribunal.

SR

Sir John Elliot, FCIT

Joined SR in 1925 as Assistant to the General Manager, Public Relations and Advertising. Assistant to Traffic Manager for Development of Traffic, 1930. Assistant Traffic Manager, 1933. Assistant General Manager, 1937. Deputy General Manager, 1940. General Manager (acting), 1947. Chief Regional Officer, Southern Region, 1948–50. Transport Adviser (Railways), Government of Victoria, Australia, 1949. Director, Railway Air Services and Channel Islands Airways, 1937–48. Chief Regional Officer, London Midland Region, 1950. Chairman, the Railway Executive, 1951. Chairman, London Transport Executive, 1953–59. Chairman, Pullman Car Co. Ltd, 1959–63. Chairman, Thos. Cook & Son Ltd, 1959–67. Director, Cie. Internationale des Wagons-Lits, 1961–71. Vice-President, Union Internationale des Chemins de Fer (UIC), 1947–53. President, Chartered Institute of Transport, 1953. Transport Adviser, East Africa (World Bank), 1969.

J. L. Harrington, OBE, FCIT, Chevalier de la Légion d'Honneur, Officier du Mérite Maritime (France); Chevalier of the Order of Leopold (Belgium)

Educated University College School, London. Joined SR, 1924. After service in Traffic Department, appointed a cadet for training, including a period with the London Underground. Assistant to the Traffic Manager, 1934. Divisional Marine Manager, Dover, 1938. General Assistant to General Manager, 1941. Chief Officer (Administration), the Railway Executive, 1948. Chief Officer (Marine and Administration), 1951. Chief Shipping and International Services Officer, British Transport Commission, 1956. General Manager (Shipping and International Services) British Railways Board, 1963. Deputy Chairman, British Rail Shipping and International Services Board, 1970. Retired 1971.

London Transport

Anthony Bull, CBE, MA, FCIT

Brief Traffic Apprenticeship with Nord Railway of France, 1926. At Cambridge University 1926–29 before joining London Underground Group, 1929. Experience in Staff and Public Relations Departments and in Chairman's office, 1929–36. Personal Assistant to Vice-Chairman, London Passenger Transport Board, 1936–39. After war service, 1939–46, appointed Chief Staff and Welfare Officer, LPTB, 1946. Member of the London Transport Executive for Staff and Welfare, 1955 and later also for the LT railways. Vice-Chairman, London Transport Board and then London Transport Executive, 1965–71. President of the Chartered Institute of Transport, 1969–70. Retired 1971. Subsequently consultant on overseas transport projects.

Railway Clearing House

T. J. Lynch

Joined Railway Clearing House as Probationer, 1909. Junior clerkship, Mileage and Demurrage Section, 1910. War service, 1914–19. General clerical duties, Secretarial Department, RCH, 1919. Loaned to LNWR, 1920. General clerical duties, RCH, 1921. Junior Committee Secretary, 1923. Loaned to LNER Parliamentary Office, 1925. Committee Secretary, RCH, 1926. Head of General Duties Section (Secretariat), 1929. Senior Conference Secretary, 1940. Head of Secretarial Department, 1945. Assistant Secretary, RCH, 1956. Secretary, Railway Clearing House Corporation, 1947. Secretary, Railway Clearing House (on dissolution of

Corporation), 1955. Retired 1957.

Railway Clerks' Association

D. Robertson, JP

Joined GNSR, 1919, in Superintendent of the Line's office at Aberdeen. Transferred to Staff section, 1923, Northern Scottish Area, LNER. Resigned in 1935 to join Railway Clerks' Association as an official in the Glasgow office. Moved to RCA headquarters in London, 1939. Scottish Secretary of RCA, Glasgow, 1940. Member of General Council of the Scottish Trades Union Congress, and President of the Congress, 1947. Senior Secretarial Assistant, British Transport Commission, 1948. Principal Establishment and Staff Officer, BTC, 1957. Director of Establishment, British Railways Board, 1959. Director of Resettlement and Welfare, BRB, 1963. Retired 1968.

Railway Research Service

C. E. Whitworth, B.Com, FCIT

Graduated at London School of Economics. Studied in France and Switzerland. Joined LNER, 1928. Commercial and Operating Departments and Continental Department from 1929. Seconded to Railway Research Service as Assistant Secretary, 1939. Assistant to Chief Officer (Administration), the Railway Executive, 1949. Assistant Freight and Passenger Officer, British Transport Commission, 1954. Personal Assistant to Traffic Adviser, BTC, 1955. General Assistant to General Manager, Eastern Region, 1955. Principal Assistant to General Manager, Eastern Region, 1967. Retired 1969.

Index

References to individual railway companies are too numerous to index as they occur almost continuously throughout the text. Subjects are indicated clearly by the chapter headings.

Page numbers in ROMAN figures relate to pages of text: numbers in *italics* relate to end-of-chapter references to documents or interviews.